Communicate
Listening & Speaking Skills

Coursebook

Kate Pickering

MACMILLAN

Contents

• DVD worksheets pages 95–102   • Exam Tips page 103

Meeting up

Phrase bank

goth
skater
heavy
emo

introvert
mate
outgoing
unreliable
messy
hard-working
intense
sporty
fun-loving
strict
depressive
reserved
relaxed
understanding

really into
quite keen on
not really bothered about
can't stand

Vocabulary: describing people

1 **Label the people in the pictures using words from the Phrase bank.**

2 🔊 1/02 **Listen to one of the people from 1. Identify the speaker and complete the description in the speech bubble.**

> *Some people say I'm quite _____.*
> *I'm really into _____.*

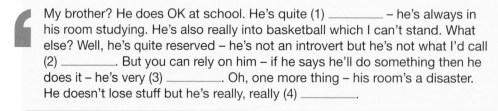

3 **Read adjectives 1–4. Find an antonym for each one in the Phrase bank.**

1 dependable _____

2 lazy _____

3 quiet _____

4 organized _____

4 🔊 1/03 **Use adjectives from 3 to complete this description. Listen and check.**

> My brother? He does OK at school. He's quite (1) _____ – he's always in his room studying. He's also really into basketball which I can't stand. What else? Well, he's quite reserved – he's not an introvert but he's not what I'd call (2) _____. But you can rely on him – if he says he'll do something then he does it – he's very (3) _____. Oh, one more thing – his room's a disaster. He doesn't lose stuff but he's really, really (4) _____.

5 **Look at the words below. Write a (+) or a (−) sign to indicate which are positive and which are negative.**

a good mate (+)   strict   a pain

relaxed   a real laugh   understanding

6 🔊 1/04 **Listen to six speakers describing people. Choose a word from 5 for each person.**

Person 1: *a pain*   Person 4:

Person 2:   Person 5:

Person 3:   Person 6:

7 **Describe someone in your family or one of your friends. Use expressions from this page.**

Culture

Traditionally, the word 'mate' was used by men to talk about male friends. Today, it is used by teenagers of both sexes to talk about male and female friends.

Speaking: discussing relationships

1 (1/05) **Listen to four dialogues. Match them to the photos.**

Dialogue 1 ___

Dialogue 2 ___

Dialogue 3 ___

Dialogue 4 ___

A. _____

B. _____

C. _____

D. _____

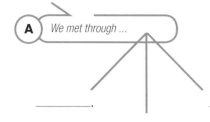

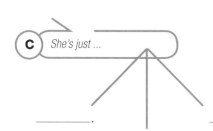

2a **Put the dialogue in the correct order. Write a number (1–8).**

Anna: Peter? This is Clare. Clare studies at York with Danny. _1_

Peter: Me? I'm his brother. ___

Peter: Peter. So are you one of Danny's judo friends? ___

Clare: No, I'm not really into sport. ___

Clare: What about you? How do you know Danny? ___

Clare: Hi, nice to meet you too. Sorry, I didn't catch your name ...

Peter: Hi Clare. Nice to meet you. ___

Anna: Clare and Danny are on the same course. ___

2b (1/06) **Listen and check.**

3 **Use words from the Phrase bank to complete A–C below in three different ways.**

A *We met through ...*

_____ . _____ .

_____ .

B *I'm one of his ...*

_____ . _____ .

C *She's just ...*

_____ . _____ .

_____ .

4 💬 **Work in pairs. Tell your partner about three people you know. Use phrases from 3 to describe your relationship.**

5 💬 **Write a dialogue introducing your partner to another friend of yours. Practise the dialogue in pairs.**

Language note

When we introduce a new person to a friend we say ...

Hi, this is Javi or

Let me introduce you to Javi

~~I present you Javi~~

Pronunciation

/eɪ/

a (1/07) **Listen to the words and note the /eɪ/ sounds.**

b **Read the words. How would you pronounce them?**

neighbour   lazy
play   pain

c (1/08) **Listen and check.**

Phrase bank

technophobe
click on
go to
set up
create
upload
join
confirm

account
register button
social networking site
email address
security question
password
question forum
social interaction
online profile

1 Do you or your friends use any of these social networking sites? If not, which do you use?

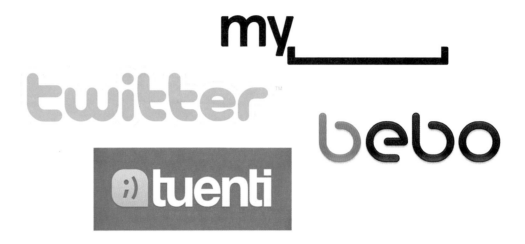

2 You are going to listen to an expert explaining how to set up a social networking account. Before you listen, predict the correct alternative for sentences 1–8.

1 The first thing to do is **set up/go to** a website, like, Facebook.

2 Then **click on/create** the register button.

3 The next step is to **upload/create** an account for yourself.

4 You then need to **choose/click on** a password.

5 You also need to **join/confirm** your email address.

6 The website will probably ask you to **set up/confirm** a security question to remind you of your password in case you forget it.

7 Once you've done that you can **upload/set up** a photo of yourself ...

8 ...or **join/upload** a forum to share opinions about something you're interested in.

3 🔘 1/09 Listen to the first part of the interview and check your answers.

4 🔘 1/10 Listen to the second part of the interview and answer the questions in your own words.

1 According to Patrick, what is the difference between the way young people and adults use social networking sites?

2 What does Patrick say about social networking and young people's social interaction?

3 What is Patrick's main concern about social networking sites?

4 Why does Richard suggest that we shouldn't be too worried about young people using social networking sites?

5 🔘 1/10 Listen again and complete the statistics.

1 number of active Facebook users ＿＿

2 age of the young people in the study ＿＿

3 proportion of young people in Britain with an online profile ＿＿%

4 percentage of young people with a Bebo profile ＿＿%

5 proportion of adults using social networking to make friends ＿＿%

6 proportion of parents who don't supervise their children's social networking ＿＿ %

Culture

People who use social networking sites often include acronyms in their messages. These have become so popular that they are sometimes used in spoken language. Examples of this 'netspeak' include:

LOL – laugh out loud

ROTF – rolling on the floor (laughing)

AFK – away from keyboard

BAK – back at keyboard

FYI – for your information

BTW – by the way

G2G – got to go

TBC – to be continued

Functional language: opinions

1 Complete the sentences from the interview about social networking using expressions from the Phrase bank.

1   Patrick Hammond is a child psychologist based here in London – Patrick _____ up-to-date with things like social networking?

2   Right, that's the Ofcom study. So Patrick _____ that?

3   So 60% of young people and only 17% of adults – _____ a problem?

4   I suppose you're right. OK, so _____ that?

5   Richard, can I bring you in at this point – _____ children and social networking?

2 Read the questions. Match an answer a–e to each question.

1   Could you tell us something about the different social groups in your school? __

2   Do you consider yourself to be a member of a particular social group? __

3   How far do you think that dressing like other people is a type of uniform? __

4   What do you think about young people having to wear school uniform? __

5   What's your opinion on the restrictions on the use of hijab and other religious symbols in schools? __

a   Well, I don't really see what the problem is. I don't think the school should interfere in personal things like religion.

b   Now I think that's ridiculous – I do not want to wear some horrible tartan skirt.

c   Me? No, I don't think so.

d   Let's see – there's quite a big group of goths in our year and quite a lot of rappers and skaters, and the rest – well, they're just kind of normal or sporty.

e   That's an interesting question. I guess it's a way of showing you belong to a group.

3 ▷ Practise reading the dialogue in 2 with a partner.

4 Think of how you would answer the questions in 2.

5 ▷ Work in pairs. Ask and answer the questions in 2.

Final task: asking someone's opinion

1 🎧 1/11 **Look at the cartoon. Try to predict how the teacher's questions might end. Listen and check.**

2 **Match the questions to the answers. Does the parent (P) or teacher (T) ask each question?**

1 What types of things ...?

2 How often do you ...?

3 What's your opinion on ...?

a ... check he has done his homework?

b ... letting teenagers organize their own time?

c ... do you think I could do to change his routines?

3 🎧 1/11 **Listen again and check your answers.**

4 💬 **Work in pairs to interview a partner about their opinions. Decide who is Student A and Student B then read your roles.**

Pronunciation

Questions

a **Read the question below. Does it require an open response or a yes / no response?**

Is your partner a good student?

b 🎧 1/12 **Listen to the question. Does the intonation rise or fall at the end of the question?**

Student A

You are the teacher of a student who doesn't study enough. You have to ask the parent's opinion about the issues below. Prepare your questions.

Issues

1 Possibly restricting access to the internet at home to certain hours

2 Possibly limiting use of electronic games

3 Possibly restricting time he spends with friends

Student B

You are the parent of a student who doesn't study enough. You want to defend your son/daughter but you don't want to appear irresponsible. Prepare your responses.

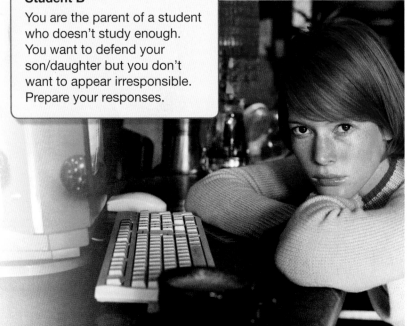

Vocabulary

1 Read the adjectives in the list and divide them into positive and negative qualities.

dependable   hard-working   lazy   messy   organized
outgoing   quiet   relaxed   strict   unreliable

2 💬 Complete the dialogue. Work in pairs. One student says an adjective from 1. The other student says the opposite adjective.

What is the opposite of dependable?
The opposite of dependable? I think it's _____

3 💬 Think of someone you both know. One student says three adjectives to describe that person. The other student must guess who it is.

4 Cross out the word that does not collocate with the verbs in blue.

click on	a button	a link	a forum
choose	a blog	a password	a security question
upload	a photo	a video	a blog
join	a forum	a link	a social networking site
create	a profile	a photo album	a button

Pronunciation

5 Underline the /eɪ/ sound in sentences 1-4.

1 I want to create a social networking account.
2 My friends and I use Myspace to organize parties.
3 I've never met anyone through speed dating.
4 I've got 80 friends on Facebook.

6 (1/13) Listen and check.

Functional language

7 Put the words in the correct order to make questions.

a to / Do / yourself / consider / you / be ... / ?
b about / Could / tell / us / you / something ... / ?
c opinion / your / What / on ... / 's / ?
d do / you / What / about ... / think / ?

8 Complete the questions in 7 with these phrases.

a restricting the hours that teenagers spend on the internet
b the different ways you use computers
c people downloading music and videos
d computer literate

9 💬 Work in pairs. Take turns to ask and answer the questions in 7.

Phrase bank

goth skater
heavy emo
introvert mate
unreliable
hard-working
outgoing messy
intense sporty
fun-loving strict
depressive
reserved relaxed
understanding
really into
quite keen on
not really bothered
    about
can't stand

... a girl from my class
... a mutual friend
classmates
neighbours
one of my parents'
    friends
... someone I know
    from football/judo/
    the orchestra

technophobe
click on go to
set up create
upload join
confirm an account
register button
social networking site
email address
security question
password
question forum
social interaction
online profile

Do you consider
    yourself to be ...?
Could you tell us
    something about ...?
How far do you think
    that's ...?
What's your opinion
    on ...?
What do you think
    about ...?

Phrase bank

A levels
apprenticeship
vocational training
sixth form
further education
sandwich course
work experience
vacancies
placement

stay on
enrol on
apply for
take on

Culture

In Britain, the last two years of school are called **sixth form**.

Pre-university qualifications are called **A levels**.

School-based preparation for work is called **vocational training**.

Work-based training of young employees is called an **apprenticeship**.

Language note

We often use 'take' when talking about a choice of school or university subject.

I want to take a psychology degree at university.

I'm taking Spanish instead of French this year.

Vocabulary: leaving school

1 🔘 1/14 **Listen to three 17-year-olds. Use their names to complete the descriptions.**

1 _____ is a sixth former.

2 _____ is doing a training course.

3 _____ is a school leaver.

Dean

Jo

Gemma

2 **Which of the people in 1 mentions …**

1 a sandwich course? _____

2 a degree? _____

3 work experience? _____

3 🔘 1/15 **Listen to Jo, Gemma and Dean. How are their lives different now to when they were at school? Write one similarity and one difference for each person.**

	similarities	differences
Jo		
Gemma		
Dean		

4 **Complete the speech bubbles below with words from the box.**

> vocational training   apprenticeships   vacancies   A levels

5 **Match the blue words in the speech bubbles to synonyms 1–4.**

1 request _____

2 join _____

3 remain _____

4 recruit _____

3 There aren't many _____ at the moment and hundreds of people apply for each one.

1 I've decided to stay on at school to take _____.

4 Some companies take on school leavers to do _____. They're great – you get paid while you learn!

2 My mum convinced me to enrol on a _____ course, I want to learn to be a hotel manager.

Speaking: talking about choices

1 Read the school subjects in the Phrase bank. Which are compulsory and which are optional for you?

2 🔊 1/16 Listen to two friends Alex and Rhona compare their school experiences. Complete the table for them.

Who	Alex	Rhona
studies nine subjects?		
studies four subjects?		
is studying humanities?		
wants to take business studies?		

Alex

3 Are the statements true (T) or false (F)?

1 Rhona thinks the British and Spanish systems are similar. ___

2 Alex has official exams this year. ___

3 There are compulsory A level subjects. ___

4 Maths, physics and chemistry are compulsory for Jimena. ___

4a Match the two parts of the expressions.

1 How does it   **a** for a specific job.

2 You have to   **b** humanities.

3 You can train   **c** choose an option.

4 I've opted for   **d** work in your school?

4b 🔊 1/17 Listen and check.

Rhona

5 Read part of what Alex and Rhona said. Complete the dialogue with words from the box.

crazy	useless	subjects	primary	opted	sciences	option

R: OK, take my friend Jimena for example. She's doing _____ so she had to take maths, physics and chemistry ... no choice, they're compulsory ... but then she can either do biology or technical drawing plus one more _____.

A: And you? Which _____ are you doing?

R: Oh, I'm _____ at science; I want to be a _____ school teacher, so I've_____ for humanities. I had to do Greek, Latin and history, and then I could choose between French, ICT and history of music.

A: OK, so which did you choose?

R: French.

A: French! You're _____!

6 💬 Rewrite the dialogue so that it is true for you and a friend. Have a conversation with your partner.

Example: *You know my friend Javi? Well, he's taking ...*

Phrase bank

art
Latin
Greek
citizenship
ICT
PE
maths
biology
physics
chemistry
technical drawing
history
history of music
French
business studies
health studies
the British system
humanities
sciences

Pronunciation

Initial 's'

a Read the phrases aloud. How do you pronounce the words in blue?

a business **studies** degree
the **Spanish** system
a **specific** type of job
She's doing health **studies**

b 🔊 1/18 Listen and check.

Phrase bank

A levels
apprenticeship
vocational training
sixth form
further education
sandwich course
work experience
vacancies
placement

Listening: careers advice

1 🔘 **1/19 Listen to an interview between a careers advisor and a sixth form student. Answer the questions.**

1 Why does the advisor ask Tara about her interests?

2 What kind of career does he think would suit Tara?

2 🔘 **1/19 Listen again and choose the correct answer.**

1 Tara ...
  a doesn't like any subjects at school.
  b likes some subjects, but not others.
  c likes all her school subjects.

2 Tara ...
  a wants to buy a video camera in the future.
  b doesn't have a camera now.
  c is saving to buy a better camera.

3 Tara ...
  a wants to do vocational training.
  b wants to look for a job after school.
  c knows her parents want her to go to university.

4 Mr Lee asks Tara to ...
  a make a decision.
  b go home.
  c come back to talk about it some more.

Culture

A careers advisor helps students decide what to do after secondary school.

Useful language

*On the one hand ...
on the other hand*

However, ...

Yet, ...

Some people think ...

While I agree that's a good idea, I think ...

3 💬 **Work in pairs. Discuss the pros and cons of the sources of careers advice below. Use the expressions in the Useful language box.**

1 Researching options on the internet.
2 Talking to a careers advisor.
3 Talking to your parents or other family members.
4 Talking to your friends.
5 Doing a test to evaluate your suitability for different jobs.
6 Doing the same job your parents do.

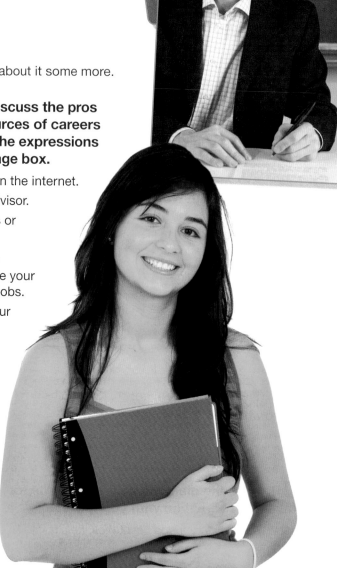

CAREERS ADVISOR

Functional language: advice

1 Look at the words and phrases in the Phrase bank. Complete the table with the expressions.

Asking for information	Saying what you like or what you're good/bad at	Making suggestions
• *How are you getting on with?* •	• •	• •
Reacting to a suggestion	**Giving advice**	**Saying something is not a good idea**
• • •	• •	•

2 Complete the sentences so they are true for you.

1 I'm quite good at _____ .

2 My best friend is really into _____ .

3 I'd had enough of _____ so I'm not studying it this year.

4 If you want to be a _____ (a profession), you should _____ .

5 If you're into _____ (a sport), it's a good idea to _____ .

3 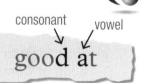 Work in pairs. One of you will be a careers advisor and the other a student. Use expressions from 1 for your interview.

Student A

You are a careers advisor. Write four or five questions you could ask in order to find out about Student B's abilities and plans.

Student B

You are a student. Think of two subjects you're good at, two that you dislike and two things you do in your free time. Ask Student A for careers advice.

Phrase bank

How are you getting on with …?
I'm useless at …
You should do …
I think I've had enough of …
It's a good idea to …
What do you like doing in your free time?
I'm really into …
Maybe something like …?
I'm quite good at …
Sounds OK
I wouldn't recommend …
I don't know …
Cool!
I hate …
Why don't you have a think about it?

Pronunciation

consonant   vowel

good at

Word linking

a 1/20 **Listen to the blue words in the phrases below. Can you hear two words or one?**

I'm **good at** English.
I'm **useless at** physics.
I've **had enough** of physics.
It's a **good idea**.
Have a **think about it**.

b Practise linking the final and initial sounds in each pair of words.

Final task: an interview

1 💬 **Work in pairs. Read the advert. When you finish, close your book and tell your partner what you remember.**

Camp Sur needs
YOU!

Camp Sur, based in a village near Salamanca, will welcome young people aged 15–18 from Britain, Holland, Denmark and Germany during the month of July.

We need:
young people of the same age whose first language is Spanish to take part in the camp. All you have to do is to speak Spanish during all meal-times and social activities.

We offer:
- free board and accommodation
- free participation in a range of sporting and social activities
- the opportunity to meet other teenagers from a range of European countries.

Interviews at the Hotel Vista Cibeles, Madrid – April 10th and 11th.

2 🎧 (1/21) **Listen to an interview with a candidate for a job at Camp Sur then answer the questions.**

1 What impression did she give?
2 How did the interviewer feel about the candidate?
3 What advice would you give this candidate?

3 💬 **Work in pairs to carry out an interview for a job at Camp Sur. Follow the instructions below.**

Strategy

Choose an option to complete the advice for interview candidates.

When talking about yourself in an interview …

1 **express/don't express** an interest in the interviewer's questions.

2 **give/avoid giving** short, one or two word, answers.

3 **use/avoid using** the phrase 'I don't know'.

Student A
You work for Camp Sur. Ask about …
- what the candidate is doing at school now.
- the academic choices the candidate has made.
- the candidate's future plans for study and/or work.
- the candidate's interests and hobbies.
- why the candidate is interested in working at Camp Sur.

Student B
You are a candidate for a place at Camp Sur. Prepare to give information about …
- your studies now and in the past.
- your future plans for study and/or work.
- your hobbies and interests.
- why you're interested in working at Camp Sur.
- what you can offer Camp Sur.
- any questions you have about the camp.

Vocabulary

1 Write the words in a logical sequence. There may be more than one possible answer.

1   sixth form   university   primary school   work   secondary school

_____

2   do a degree   leave school   do a subject   have a career   pass an exam

_____

2 Cross out the odd one out in each group.

1   careers advisor / school leaver / teacher
2   vocational training / work experience / sixth form
3   degree / optional / compulsory
4   sixth form / further education / university

3 (1/22) Listen and number the items in the order you hear them defined.

careers advisor _____

vocational training _____

secondary school _____

A levels _____

compulsory _____

4 Write the words in order to complete the subject definitions. Write a subject for each definition.

1   In this subject learn/students/about/computers/how/work. _____

2   This subject how/system/the/teaches/economic/functions. _____

3   In this subject students/physical/the/about/of/importance/learn/exercise. _____

4   This subject society/about/own/students/teaches/their. _____

Pronunciation

5a Mark the words that link together.

1   I work in a school.
2   I'm not a teacher.
3   I hate exams.
4   Have a talk about it.

5b (1/23) Listen and check.

Functional language

6 Read the task box and complete the conversation.

> **Task**   After a term studying sciences, Julia decides she doesn't like it. She asks her best friend for advice.
>
> Write a dialogue between Julia and her best friend. Use the Phrase bank to help you.

Phrase bank

A levels
apprenticeship
vocational training
sixth form
further education
sandwich course
work experience
vacancies
placement

stay on   enrol on
apply for   take on

art   Latin
Greek   citizenship
ICT   PE
maths   biology
physics
chemistry
technical drawing
history
history of music
French
business studies
health studies
the British system
humanities
sciences

How are you getting
   on with …?
I'm useless at …
You should do …
I think I've had
   enough of …
It's a good idea to …
What do you like doing
   in your free time?
I'm really into …
Maybe something
   like …?
I'm quite good at …
Sounds OK
I wouldn't
   recommend …
I don't know …
Cool!
I hate …
Why don't you have a
   think about it?

 Now watch the DVD episode Leaving school   **15**

Study abroad

Vocabulary: booking a course

1 1/24 **Listen to a student describe her study trip to England. Which four things from the Phrase bank does she mention?**

2 **Imagine you are going to study abroad. Complete the online registration form using words from the Phrase bank.**

It's as easy as A, B, C. Choose from one of the following accommodation options:

A Many students prefer the (1) _____ option, because living in an English home gives you first-hand experience of English life.

B For the student who prefers a less intensive time, the (2) _____ option on a university campus is ideal.

C The more independent student may prefer a (3) _____. Although this is more expensive, many enjoy the freedom it brings.

With A or B you can choose from the following catering options: (4) _____ (all meals provided) or (5) _____ (breakfast/evening meal only).

Option C is (6) _____ only.

When you make a reservation, you pay an **enrolment fee**. This acts as a **deposit**, and guarantees your place on the course.

The **balance** of your fees is payable on arrival at the school. **Course fees** are normally all-inclusive.

You may be eligible for a **grant** from the European Union to pay for your studies.

3 **Read Step 2 of the form. Use the words in bold to complete the definitions for ways of paying for a course.**

1 A proportion of the total cost paid to reserve goods or services is a _____.

2 Help from an official body to pay for the cost of a course is a _____.

3 An _____ is what you pay to join a course.

4 The complete cost of a programme of study is the _____.

5 Following an initial payment, the _____ is the rest of the money you need to pay.

Speaking: discussing preferences

1 🔊 **1/25 Listen and identify speakers 1-4. Find words in the Phrase bank to label each speaker.**

1 Speaker 1 is _____
2 Speaker 2 is _____
3 Speaker 3 is _____
4 Speaker 4 is _____

2 🔊 **1/25 Listen to the speakers again and decide if the statements are true or false.**

1 Speaker 1 offers full-board accommodation with a host family. ___
2 Sarah Johnson deals with students' accommodation problems. ___
3 The person responsible for taking payment from students is Margaret. ___
4 Dirk thinks that there are advantages to staying with a host family. ___

3 Imagine you are going to study in Brighton and you want to know more about accommodation options. Which of speakers 1-4 would you talk to?

4 🔊 **1/26 Listen to Speaker 4 discussing his preferences. Complete what he says with words from the Phrase bank, then choose the best alternative in bold.**

1 Some students **prefer/preferred** the host family option. It's a _____ learning English.
2 Maybe it's _____ you if you feel homesick, too.
3 My parents **would prefer/prefer** me to stay with a host family.
4 _____ staying in a hall of residence is that you have your own room.
5 **I rather/I'd rather** have some _____ than live in a family situation.
6 I think what **I like/I'd like** _____ would be to share an apartment!

5 💬 **Work in pairs. Use the phrases in 4 to talk about where you would prefer to stay if you were studying abroad.**

Phrase bank

Director of Studies
host family member
language student
language school
  receptionist

great way of
most of all
good for
personal space
the thing I like about …

I'd rather stay …
I prefer living …
  alone / with other
  people / in a homely
  environment

Pronunciation

/s/ and /ʃ/
sounds

a 🔊 1/27 **Listen and identify the word you hear.**

show / so
share / Sarah
sign / shine
see / she

Phrase bank

level test
native speaker
sporting and cultural
    activities
guided tours
daily timetable
flexible
optional
conversation classes
business English
survival English
general English
young learners course

1a Javi is going to call a language school. Read his questions. Which could he answer by reading the advert?

1b 1/28 Listen and answer the rest of the questions.

Remember to ask

* How do you get to Brighton?
* Brighton? What is there to do there?
* Are there different courses available?
* Number of students per group?
* Do they arrange accommodation?
* How to book course?
* Contact name?

Brighton Academy of English

- Fantastic coastal location
- 2 ½ hrs by road or train from London; international airport
- Well-equipped self-access centre
- Wifi and student social area
- Varied social programme including weekend excursions
- Range of accommodation options
- Competitive prices

www.brightonacademyofenglish.com

Culture

Brighton is also known as London-by-the-sea, because so many Londoners live there and commute to work by train.

Pronunciation

/ɔː/

a 1/29 Listen to the words. Which have the sound /ɔː/?

hour   hall   abroad
half-board   four

b 1/29 Listen again and repeat the words.

2 1/28 **Listen again and choose the correct answer for each question.**

1 Which course does the receptionist recommend for the caller?

  a Business English

  b Young Learners course

  c Survival English

  d General English

2 What does the receptionist say about the length of courses?

  a Most students stay for a month.

  b Students can study for as long as they want.

  c You have to stay for at least a week.

  d Courses last most of the summer.

3 What's the timetable like for students at the school?

  a It's completely flexible.

  b The afternoon is optional.

  c It's divided equally between morning and afternoon.

  d Students have three hours of class in the morning and two hours in the afternoon.

4 What are the accommodation options for students?

  a They must stay with a host family.

  b The school organizes the student's preferred option.

  c Most students stay with a family at first and then go to the hall of residence.

  d Students can choose where they want to stay.

3 **Which of the courses in the Phrase bank would be useful for you?**

Functional language: phone calls

1 Copy the table into your notebook. Then complete it using the expressions in the Phrase bank.

Offering to help	Clarifying what the customer wants	Confirming
• What would you like to know? • •	• What type of course are you interested in? •	• Yes, of course • • •
Explaining what you want	**Asking for information**	**Checking**
• I was phoning for some information about your school. • • •	• Can you tell me something about where the school is? • • •	• All the teachers are native speakers, right? •

2 Add the expressions to the correct box in the table in 1.

What kind of accommodation were you thinking of?

That's right. What can I do for you?

Can you tell me more about the options available?

I'm interested in hearing about the accommodation you offer.

Is that Brighton Academy?

3 Look at the sentences in 2. Decide whether it is the caller (C) or the receptionist (R) who says each sentence. Complete the dialogue in the speech bubbles below.

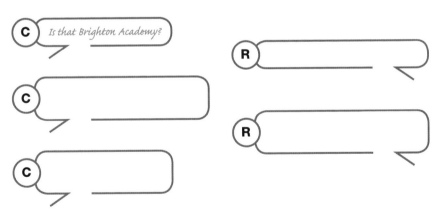

C — Is that Brighton Academy?

R

C

R

C

4 🗨 Work in pairs. Decide who is Student A and Student B. Use the Phrase bank to help you complete the task.

Student A

You are a receptionist in a language school. Think about the services and facilities your school offers. Answer Student A's questions.

Student B

You are a student. You want to call a language school to enquire about the following:

• The cost of general English courses

• Things to do in the area

• Types of course available

Call the receptionist at the school.

Phrase bank

certainly

How can I help you?

How many hours of classes are there per day?

I'm interested in a group class.

OK, sure.

What about social activities – do you have anything like that?

What about the courses on offer?

Could you tell me how much … costs?

Culture 🌐

To identify yourself on the phone in English, or to check the identity of a caller, use the third person.

It's Maria.

~~I am Maria.~~

Is that John?

~~Are you John?~~

Final task: talking about priorities

1 Read the facilities and services a language school offers. Which are the most important?

airport transfer

daily social programme

cafeteria

wifi access

excursions and outings

good public transport

located in a big city

native speaker teachers

Strategy

When you discuss priorities with a partner, listen to the reasons they give for their choice before giving your opinion.

2 (1/30) Read the strategy box then listen to a pair of students trying to prioritize the facilities in 1. Which speaker listens more effectively? Why?

3 💬 Work in pairs to discuss the importance of each facility. Try to prioritize them from 1 (most important) to 8 (least important).

4 Join with another pair to form a group of four. Together try to choose the four most important facilities.

5 💬 Present your ideas to the class using expressions from the Useful language box. Remember to explain your reasons.

Useful language

I think X is less important than …

I think Y is more important than …

the most important

the least important

We chose X because

We think that Y is one of the top four facilities because …

Vocabulary

1 (1/31) **Listen to the words and write each one in the correct column in the table.**

accommodation	courses	money	people

2 **Work in pairs. Add one more expression to each column.**

Pronunciation

3 (1/32) **Listen to the words and write them under the correct headings.**

study   fashion   attention   course   English   session

/s/	/ʃ/

Functional language

4 **Put the dialogue between a receptionist and a student in the correct order. Write a number (1-13).**

Student: I was interested in some information about your English classes. _1_

Receptionist: A maximum of eight. ___

Receptionist: Fine, we have First Certificate courses starting next month. Is that a group class or individual? ___

Receptionist: OK, so we have a range of courses – intensive, extensive, general and exam classes. ___

Receptionist: Sure, well we have daily group classes on our intensive programme. ___

Receptionist: Well, individual classes cost €35 an hour. ___

Receptionist: What would you like to know?. _2_

Student: Oh good, I'm interested in preparing the First Certificate exam. ___

Student: Ah, well maybe group classes then. ___

Student: Err, individual I think – how much is that? ___

Student: First of all I wanted to know what different courses you have. ___

Student: How many students are in the group? ___

Student: That sounds great, thanks. I'll think about it and get back to you. _13_

5 (1/33) **Listen and check.**

6 💬 **In pairs, practise the dialogue.**

Phrase bank

apprehensive
excited   relieved
meet new people
feel homesick
learn about another
  culture
miss friends
different food
too expensive
host family
hall of residence
shared apartment
half board
full board
self-catering
registration
enrolment fee
deposit   balance
course fees   grant

Director of Studies
host family member
language student
language school
  receptionist

great way of
most of all   good for
personal space
The thing I like about…

conversation classes
business English
survival English
general English
young learners course

certainly
How can I help you?
How many hours of
  classes are there
  per day?
I'm interested in a
  group class.
OK, sure.
What about social
  activities?
Could you tell me how
  much … costs?

 Now watch the DVD episode Leaving home   **21**

4 Shopping

Phrase bank

shop assistant
window-shopper
manager
customer
store detective
shoplifter

newsagent
factory outlet
stationer
chemist
supermarket
pound shop
post office
health food shop
convenience store

accessories
kitchenware
perfumery
food hall
shelf
receipt
price tag
aisle
trolley
cash point

Culture

In Britain, a shop that sells very cheap household items is called a pound shop.

Bargains can be bought here for about £1.

Language note

| shop | store |
| cashpoint | ATM |

Vocabulary: the high street

1 Label the people in the pictures on this page. Use words from the Phrase bank.

2 (1/34) Listen to four dialogues. Where do they take place? Use words from the Phrase bank.

Dialogue 1 is in a _____.
Dialogue 2 is in a _____.
Dialogue 3 is in a _____.
Dialogue 4 is in a _____.

1. _____   2. _____   3. _____

3 (1/35) Complete the sentences using the words below. Listen and check.

shelf   receipt   aisle   trolley

1 Chewing gum? It's on the _____ down there.
2 Sure, you'll find cleaning products in the next _____.
3 Hi, could you change this £5 note for me? I need a pound coin for the shopping _____.
4 It's true, look at the _____. These jeans only cost me £20!

4 Where can you buy the items on the shopping list? Write the department and floor.

4. _____

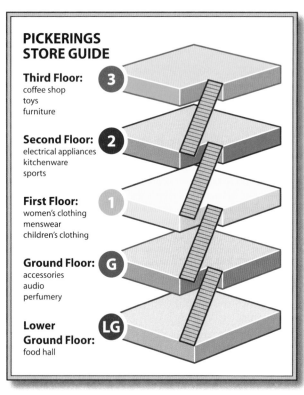

PICKERINGS STORE GUIDE

Third Floor: 3
coffee shop
toys
furniture

Second Floor: 2
electrical appliances
kitchenware
sports

First Floor: 1
women's clothing
menswear
children's clothing

Ground Floor: G
accessories
audio
perfumery

Lower Ground Floor: LG
food hall

1 digital camera _____
2 socks for Pete _____
3 music CD for party _____
4 vegetables _____
5 kitchen chair _____
6 frying pan _____
7 handbag _____

Speaking: asking for information

1 Find words in the Phrase bank to label the photos.

1. _____
2. _____
3. _____

2 (1/36) **Put the sentences about a shopping trip in a logical order. Write a number (1-4). Listen and check.**

Excuse me, could you tell me where the cameras are? _1_

No, I'm just looking, thanks. ___

Cameras? They'll be in electrical appliances – take that escalator over there. ___

Hi, would you like any help? ___

3 (1/37) **Listen to a dialogue between a customer and two members of staff in a shop. Decide if the sentences are true or false.**

1 The shop assistant says that the Fuji camera is more practical to use. ___

2 The checkout assistant says that if the customer has a problem he should return the camera to the company that made it. ___

4 Complete the conversation between a customer (C) and shop assistant (SA) with words from the Phrase bank. Use the clues in brackets to help you.

C Excuse me, could you tell me a bit about the difference between these two cameras?

SA OK, well they're pretty similar in price but the Fuji's a little (1) _____ (price), which is good! It's also a bit (2) _____ (weight) so it's easier to carry.

C What else – what about the features?

SA Let's see – well, the screen on the Canon is 2.7 inches and the Fuji's a little (3) _____ (size), which makes it easier to see what you're shooting.

C And what about resolution?

SA I think they're both 10 megapixels.

C And what about the zoom?

SA There's quite a difference there. The Canon is a compact camera, so it's only got a 4x optical zoom, but the Fuji's a bit (4) _____ (age) so it gives you the latest 15x zoom.

5 💬 Work in pairs. Practise reading the dialogue in 4 then write a similar one about two models of another appliance. Use words from the Phrase bank.

Phrase bank

lift
escalator
meeting point
checkout

sound quality
weight
design
memory capacity
special offers
credit card
cash

lighter heavier
more expensive
cheaper
smaller bigger
more traditional
more modern

Language note

In shops in Britain, if a shop assistant asks you if you want any help you can say,

No thanks, I'm just looking.

Pronunciation 🔊

/ʊ/

a (1/38) **Say the words in blue. Which letter is silent? Listen and check.**

Could you tell me where the cameras are?

Would you like any help?

You **should** keep your receipt.

b (1/39) **Which words have the /ʊ/ sound? Listen and check.**

book cook wood food
good put but cut full
pull pool

Phrase bank

guarantee
credit note
cash refund
exchange
receipt

consumer
poor service
damaged goods

rights
duty
faulty
manufacturer
policy
recordings

1 Read the definitions. Find a word in the Phrase bank for 1-5.

1 Get your money back in notes and coins. _____

2 A piece of paper confirming the price of a product and the time and place where you bought it. _____

3 A promise to repair or replace a product that is faulty within a period of time.
_____

4 Get another product to replace a damaged one. _____

5 A paper giving you the right to buy another product in the same shop for the same value as a damaged product. _____

2 🔘1/40 You are going to listen to the first part of a radio programme about consumer rights. Decide if the statements are true or false. Give reasons to support your answers.

1 Paul represents the interests of shoppers and shop workers. _____

2 Paul thinks the main problem is that consumers are ignorant of their rights.
_____

3 Paul says that the first step to getting your money back is to contact the manufacturer of the faulty product. _____

4 Paul says that shops have a duty to help customers. _____

5 According to Paul, the question of how shops respond to customers depends on each shop. _____

6 Paul secretly records his shopping trip. _____

3 🔘1/41 Listen to the second part of the radio programme and answer the questions.

1 Why is Paul so sure that the problem with his camera is not due to the memory card?

2 Why doesn't Paul want the shop to repair his camera?

3 What reason does the shop assistant give for Paul not being eligible for a cash refund?

4 According to the information on this page, did the shop assistant carry out his duty to Paul? Explain your answer.

Culture

In Britain, there are no complaint forms in shops. However, consumer protection programmes are popular on TV and radio.

Functional language: complaints

1 **Write expressions from the Phrase bank for each category (1–4) below.**

1 Ways of explaining a problem (x4).
2 Suggestions for possible solutions (x4).
3 Saying how you feel and what you want (x4).
4 Enquiring about a problem (x2).

2 **(1/42) You are going to listen to a person say the same word in five different ways. Choose an adjective from the box to describe the way in which it is said each time.**

bored	surprised	doubtful	amazed	interested

1 _____   **4** _____

2 _____   **5** _____

3 _____

3 **Work in pairs. Say the following phrases. Your partner must describe your mood using the adjectives in 2.**

Can I help you?

It's on the third floor, near the computers.

I bought this last week and it's not working.

I'd like to speak to the manager.

I'd like my money back.

I'm just looking, thank you.

4 **Identify who is speaking: the customer (C) or the shop assistant (SA). Write a number (1-10) to put the sentences in a logical order.**

_SA_ Good morning. Can I help you? _1_

____ It sounds like some type of loose connection. Would you like them repaired or would you prefer an exchange? ____

____ Yes, I bought these speakers last month and they're not working properly. ____

____ When I plug them in there's a loud buzz and the sound quality's terrible. ____

____ Well, actually I'd like my money back. ____

____ I see. Have you got the receipt? ____

____ What seems to be the trouble? ____

____ I'm afraid we can't give you a cash refund – you bought them more than 15 days ago. I could give you a credit note – that way you can buy something else in the store. ____

____ Yes, here it is. ____

_C_ Oh, OK – well, I'll take that then if I can't have cash. ____

5 **Work in pairs. Invent a similar dialogue about another faulty product. Decide how polite you want to be.**

Phrase bank

This product is faulty.
What's wrong with it?
When I turn it on nothing happens.
It doesn't do anything.
I can't hear anything.
It could be the battery.
Try rebooting it.
This isn't good enough.
I want something done about it.
What seems to be the problem?
We can send it off to be repaired.
We can give you a credit note.
No really, I'd like my money back.
I'm really not too happy about this.

Useful language

In English, to complain, we use the polite form

I'd like to speak to the manager …

even when we are angry.

Pronunciation

Expressing mood

a (1/43) **Listen to three things the sales assistant says in the dialogue on page 24.**

'Oh dear, what seems to be the trouble?'

'Oh I see. Well, if you've got the receipt we can give you a credit note.'

'Right, well, if you're sure.'

b **Practise using the same intonation.**

c **How does he sound?**

Final task: making a complaint

1 Work in pairs. Choose Option 1 or 2 then decide who is Student A and B. Read your tasks.

2 Use the Useful language box and the Phrase bank on page 25 to write notes for a dialogue. Carry out the task.

Option 1

Student A

You bought a phone two weeks ago. It doesn't work and you want a cash refund.

- Make a list of the problems.
- Think how to start the conversation.
- Decide how polite to be.

Ask the shop assistant for a refund.

Student B

You are an experienced sales assistant. Your boss has instructed you not to give any cash refunds.

- Make a list of the options you can offer to avoid giving a refund.
- Think how to start the conversation.
- Decide how polite to be.

Option 2

Student A

You bought a computer recently, but you dropped it and it doesn't work properly. You want to return it and exchange it for another one.

- Are you going to tell the truth?
- Think how to start the conversation.
- Decide how polite to be.

Ask the shop assistant for an exchange.

Student B

You work in a shop. Some computers have been returned with software problems. However, it is unusual for computers to be damaged when customers buy them. You can only exchange a computer if you are sure it was damaged when the customer bought it.

- Make a list of questions you can ask to decide if the customer is telling the truth.
- Think how to start the conversation.
- Decide how polite to be.

Useful language

What seems to be the problem?

There's a problem with …

It doesn't work.

How can I help you?

I'd like a cash refund, please.

Can you call the manager, please?

Strategy

a Remember, when speaking we can express our mood by:

- the language we use
- the intonation we use
- the body language we use

b When doing your task, try to think about:

- how you look at the other speaker
- the intonation you use
- whether to use 'please' and 'thank you'
- how direct your language is
- what you do with your hands and arms while you speak

Vocabulary

1 Add three more words from the Phrase bank to each list.

1 type of shop: supermarket

_____ _____ _____

2 departments: menswear

_____ _____ _____

3 things in a shop: bag

_____ _____ _____

2 Complete the advice for shoppers below with words from the Phrase bank.

When you buy a product in a shop, always ask for and keep the (1) _____. This has the date on it which helps you calculate the period of the (2) _____, which is normally six months to two years. If the product is faulty, you are entitled to a (3) _____ for the full price you paid. If the product works but you don't like it, you can't always get your money back but the shop may give you an (4) _____ for a similar product or a (5) _____ – which you can use to buy something of equal value in the same shop.

Pronunciation

3 (1/44) Listen to the words and identify the one you hear in each pair. Practise saying the words with your partner.

would / good   full / fool   pool / pull   should / could   to school / two schools

Functional language

4 Put the words in the correct order to make sentences.

1 Explaining a problem:

  a motor / the / I / it's / think / . _____

  b not / It's / properly / working / . _____

  c problem / with / There's / sound / a / the / . _____

2 Explaining how you feel and what you want:

  a happy / I'm / this / really / too / not / about / . _____

  b I'd / back / like / money / my / . _____

  c refund / actually / a / Well / I'd / like / cash / . _____

3 Offering solutions:

  a note / can / give / a / We / you / credit / . _____

  b off / repaired / send / We / can / it / to / be / . _____

  c exchange / you / Would / like / an / ? _____

5 Read the task box and write a dialogue.

> **Task** Think of something you bought recently. Think of something that might go wrong with it.
>
> Write a conversation between yourself and a shop assistant. Use the Phrase bank to help you.

Phrase bank

shop assistant
window shopper
manager
customer
store detective
shoplifter
newsagent
factory outlet
stationer chemist
supermarket
pound shop
post office
health food shop
convenience store
accessories
kitchenware
perfumery
food hall shelf
receipt price tag
aisle trolley
cash point

lift escalator
meeting point
till sound quality
weight design
memory capacity
heavier
cheaper bigger
More traditional
More modern

guarantee
credit note
checkout
cash refund
exchange
receipt

This product is faulty.
What's wrong with it?
When I turn it on
  nothing happens.
It doesn't do anything.
I can't hear anything.
It could be the battery.
Try rebooting it.
This isn't good enough.
I want something done
  about it.
What seems to be the
  problem?

 Now watch the DVD episode Appearances

Prepare to ...
describe a photo

1 (1/45) **Look at the photos of places where people go on holiday. Listen to someone describing one of them. Which one is it?**

2 Tick the things the speaker does

- refers to how the photo makes him feel ☐
- talks about where things are in the photo ☐
- talks in detail about what he can see ☐
- tries to use descriptive language ☐
- draws his own conclusions and makes deductions ☐

3 Look at the photos again then write A or B to indicate which photo you associate with each word.

serene ___   overcrowded ___   holidaymakers ___   unspoilt ___

packed ___   nature-lovers ___   filthy ___   breathtaking scenery ___

sunshade ___   peaceful ___   shoreline ___   paddling ___

4 (1/46) **Listen to two more students describe photos A and B. How are their descriptions different from the first student's? Use the ideas in 2 to help you.**

5 (1/46) **Listen again and decide if the statements are true or false. Give reasons to support your answers.**

Photo A

1 The speaker would like to be in the photo.

2 The speaker talks about individuals in the photo.

3 The speaker thinks the scene could be in Brazil.

4 The speaker doesn't like beach holidays.

Photo B

1 The speaker likes this scene.

2 The speaker thinks it's definitely a European scene.

3 The speaker thinks the people are tourists.

6 **Read the words for describing places. Write them under the appropriate headings.**

exciting   noisy   car horns   tense   crowded   stadium
powerful sound-system   chanting   pollution   booing   pitch   supporters
frustrating   stressful   amazing lights   at a standstill   cheering

a football match	a traffic jam	a disco

7 💬 **Work in pairs. Decide who is Student A and Student B. Use the Useful language to help you complete the task.**

Student A

Describe photo 1.

Describe the place and speculate about what might be happening.

Student B

Describe photo 2.

Describe the place and give an opinion about it.

5

Prepare to...
give an opinion

1 🗩 **Work in pairs. One of you think of ten reasons for living in a city. The other, think of ten reasons for living in a village.**

2 🗩 **Together, discuss the advantages and disadvantages of living in each place.**

3 (1/47) **Listen to James talking about why he likes his city. Which city does he live in?**

4 **Tick the reasons he gives for wanting to live there.**

1 The city's fascinating past ☐
2 Its excellent transport network ☐
3 Modern aspects of the city ☐
4 Its multicultural population ☐
5 Opportunities for employment ☐
6 Attractions for tourists ☐
7 Shopping ☐
8 Famous sporting venues ☐

5 (1/47) **Read specific examples of what James likes about his city. Write 1-8 to indicate which of the things in 4 they relate to. Listen and check.**

architecture ___ Camden Lock market ___
districts with international atmosphere ___ fashion ___
food from round the world ___ museums ___
Oxford Street ___ Shakespeare's Globe theatre ___
sightseeing ___ The Tower of London ___

6 **Complete the table below with words and phrases from the Useful language box.**

getting around	opportunities	pace of life	being at the heart of things

Useful language

a selection of universities and colleges
international communications hub
commuters
congestion
fast-moving
good prospects of employment
headquarters of organisations and
businesses
high pressure
local public transport network
range of leisure facilities
rush hour
seat of central government
stressful
variety of entertainment options

7 In pairs, decide which of the things in 6 are positive aspects of city life, which are negative and which are irrelevant? Write your answers below.

positive	negative	irrelevant

8 James uses expressions to do the following things. Write one example from the audioscript on page 104 for 1-6 below.

1 Show his personal connection with the city.

2 Ask rhetorical questions.

3 Suggest things to do in the city.

4 Introduce arguments in sequence

5 Use a quotation to support his opinion

6 Give concrete reasons to support an opinion

9 Match expressions for linking ideas to their more informal equivalents.

Formal linking expressions

1 first of all

2 additionally

3 moreover

4 in terms of disadvantages

5 however, in my opinion

Informal linking expressions

a I also think

b are there any negative points?

c but for me

d to start off with

e another reason is

10 Which of the linking expressions in 9 do we use in spoken language?

Useful language

OK, well I'm from here so I'm a bit biased

What makes it so great?

Are there any negative points?

Two places I'd really recommend are …

You can find food from many different countries here.

As the famous English author said …

To start with, it's … But it's also … as well as great clubs there's live venues too … Another reason I love it is …

Task

A Prepare a speech called 'What makes my city/town/village great.'

B Work in pairs. Follow the instructions below. Make notes but don't write your speech out in full.

Write a list of five or six reasons to support your opinion

Think of real examples to support your points

Decide which linkers to use

C Listen to the other speeches. Who presents the most convincing arguments?

Prepare to...
do a project

1 (1/48) **Listen to three people talking about a weekend break. Number the photos in the order you hear them.**

2 (1/49) **We asked each person the following questions. Listen and note their answers.**

	Where did you go and why?	Are you having a good time?
Speaker 1		
Speaker 2		
Speaker 3		

3 **Read the words. Check you understand what they mean.**

department store   guided tour   sporting venue   bargain   drop into (a place)
gallery   go window shopping   the home team   posters   sightseeing   souvenirs

cultural tour	shopping trip	sporting tour

4 (1/50) **Listen to activities you might do on holiday. Write the activities under the headings in 3.**

5 💬 **Work in pairs. Discuss which type of trip you would prefer and why.**

6 In pairs, talk about holiday activities in your town or city that visitors could do. Which are the most interesting?

7 Read the project. In pairs, discuss what activities you would include in an itinerary for visitors to your city. Use the Useful language box to help you.

Project

A **Plan a weekend in your city for a group of students from another country. In pairs, discuss your answers to the questions below.**

1 Which places will you visit?
2 How will you travel between places?
3 What kind of food will you eat and where?
4 What kinds of souvenirs will you recommend visitors buy?

B **Present your weekend plan to the class. Use expressions from the Useful Language box and the ideas below to help you.**

- Decide before you start who will present each section of your plan
- Try to speak naturally from your notes rather than read them aloud
- Use visual support (posters, photos from the internet, Powerpoint)
- Make your presentation more attractive by giving your weekend a title

Useful language

Making suggestions

Why don't we (infinitive) ...?
What about (verb+ing) ...?
We could/should (infinitive)

Agreeing & disagreeing
OK, that's a good idea.
That sounds good.
No, I don't think that'll work.
That's crazy!

Confirming what you've decided
OK, so on Friday evening ...
So, first of all ...

Explaining your ideas and reasons

We decided to ...
We thought this would be a good idea because ...
We think this will appeal to visitors because ...

Describing when you're going to do things

The first thing we're going to do is ...
Later on in the day, we're going to ...
Next morning ...
On Sunday afternoon ...

6 Free time

Phrase bank

athletics
basketball
cycling
skiing
work out
aerobics
weight training
ice skating
badminton
squash
skating
swimming
hockey
martial arts
modern dance
Pilates
spinning
yoga
darts
pool
tenpin bowling
running

Useful language

Most sports or exercise activities collocate with the verbs *do*, *play* or *go*.

Work out is one of the few that doesn't require an additional verb:

She works out twice a week.

Culture

Snooker - a similar game to pool - and darts are very popular in Britain. Important championships and tournaments are broadcast to huge audiences on national television.

Vocabulary: leisure activities

1. _____
2. _____
3. _____
4. _____
5. _____

1 Label the photos with activities from the Phrase bank.

2 Try to classify the activities in 1 as games, sports or keep fit. Use the ideas below to help you.

| expends energy | no physical effort | just a bit of fun |
| develops muscle tone | improves stamina | has a clear set of rules |

3 Write five activities from the Phrase bank in the table below according to the verb used.

do	*weight training,*
play	*pool,*
go	*cycling,*

4 (1/51) Listen to five people talking about activities they do. Which activity in 1 does each speaker do?

5 (1/51) Listen again to the speakers in 4. Which speaker (1-5) ...

1 likes being able to do the sport when and where they want. ___
2 has tried different varieties of the same activity. ___
3 plays a team sport. ___
4 sees the activity as a way to relax with friends. ___
5 took up an activity to get fit. ___

6 Which of the activities in the Phrase bank are popular in your country? Do you do any of them?

Speaking: talking about hobbies

1 Look at the graphs of the most popular sports and exercise activities for 16–24-year-olds in Britain. Predict which activities are among the top five for men and for women.

snooker/pool · football · cycling · working out
swimming · aerobics · running

2 **Listen and check your predictions.**

3 Write a verb phrase from the Phrase bank for the definitions.

1 Register for a course or activity.

2 Stop doing something you have done for a period of time.

3 Start doing a new activity.

4 Learn without too much difficulty.

5 Persist in trying to do something.

6 Participate in an activity.

4 **Listen to someone describing a sport. Complete the speaker's column of the table.**

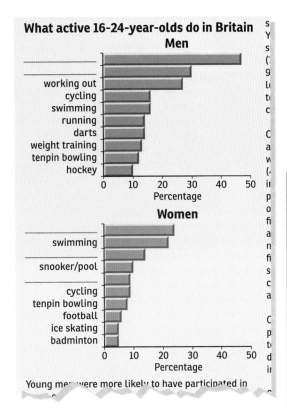

What active 16-24-year-olds do in Britain

Men

working out
cycling
swimming
running
darts
weight training
tenpin bowling
hockey

0 10 20 30 40 50
Percentage

Women

swimming
snooker/pool
cycling
tenpin bowling
football
ice skating
badminton

0 10 20 30 40 50
Percentage

Young men were more likely to have participated in ...

	speaker	you
What: the sport/activity I'm going to talk about is …		
When: I took it up …		
How long: I did it for/I've been doing it for …		
Who: I do/play it with …		
Where: I do/play it in …		
Why: I like/liked it because …		

5 Make notes in the table about a sport or activity you do now or did in the past. Work in pairs and tell each other about it.

Phrase bank

take something up
pick something up
sign up for something
stick at something
give up something
take part in something

bar
court
track
pool
gym
pitch
mountains
park

Language note

We use the verb *practise* when we work at trying to improve the way we do things, e.g.

I'm studying the piano and I practise every day.

I play tennis a couple of times a week. I've been practising my serve.

Pronunciation

Final sounds

a ▸ **Listen to the words. Pay attention to the final sound. Match the words to the correct final sound symbol.**

practises   kicks   teams

/s/   /z/   /ɪz/

b **Say the words below and write the correct final sound symbol for each one.**

aerobics   watches

dances   plays

athletics

Phrase bank

Do you fancy …
meeting up with …?
going to the cinema?
going to a gig?
playing pool/snooker/
    darts?

Useful language

When asking about what films are showing at the cinema, we ask

What's on?

When talking about the period in which a film is showing at the cinema, we say

It came out last week. or *It hasn't been out long.*

Culture

In English, it's common to make an invitation, even to a good friend, in an indirect way, using conditional sentences:

I was just wondering if you fancied …

This makes it easier for the inviter to withdraw the invitation and the invited to turn down the invitation, if necessary.

1 🔘 1/55 **Listen to two dialogues in which people are making plans to go out together. Answer the questions for each dialogue.**

	dialogue 1	dialogue 2
What is the invitation for?		
Are both speakers keen to go?		
Do they make an arrangement?		

2 🔘 1/55 **Listen again and decide if the statements are true or false.**

Dialogue 1

1 Sally's father recognizes Celia's voice. ___
2 Celia suggests more than one option. ___
3 They agree to talk again later. ___

Dialogue 2

1 Mark's mother recognizes Karl's voice. ___
2 Mark hasn't done his maths homework. ___
3 There are four free tickets. ___
4 Mark is busy earlier on Saturday. ___

3 Answer the questions.

1 In which conversation is someone evasive?
2 Do you ever react to an invitation in the way that Sally did?
3 Read the culture box. Are there any differences between the way you make invitations and the way English people do?

Functional language: making arrangements

1 (1/56) **Listen again to the beginning of the two phone conversations from page 36. In your notebook write ...**

1 two different ways to ask to speak to someone.

2 one way to ask for the name of the caller and one way to answer.

3 two ways to say you are going to pass the phone to someone.

2 Copy the table in your notebook. Complete it with expressions from the Phrase bank.

asking about plans or options	making a suggestion	making an arrangement
• •	• •	• •
being evasive	**showing enthusiasm**	**suggesting an alternative**
•	•	•

3 **Work in pairs. Choose which student to be by tossing a coin. Write a dialogue about making plans to go out.**

Student A

You want to go out with Student B. Try suggesting ...

- going to watch a sports match
- going out for something to eat

Student B

You don't mind going out with Student A but you want to suggest ...

- a different activity
- a different time

4 **Practise reading your dialogue.**

Phrase bank

I was wondering if you fancied going to the cinema tonight?
Are you free on Saturday night?
I wondered if you wanted to go...
What's on?
Could we make it a little later?
Is there anything else on?
I'll give you a call later.
We'll call for you around 7.
Oh yeah, nice one.
Great.
Mmm, maybe.
Well, I'll see.

Language note

The word *just* has several uses.

1 To ask someone to wait.

Just a moment.

2 To show that something is imminent.

He's just coming.

Pronunciation

Elision

a (1/57) **Listen to the questions. In connected speech, some sounds disappear.**

Do you want to go bowling?

Do you fancy meeting later?

b (1/57) **Listen again and repeat.**

Final task: making a date

Speakeasy

the advice website

Whether your aim is to make new friends or ask someone out on a date, your first conversation can be a real challenge. But don't worry, just try some of psychologist Samantha's simple tips, and you'll be on your way in no time.

1 Listen and ask questions
Other people like to know you're listening. By being a good listener, you let others know that you are interested in them and the things they like.

2 Keep it equal
Remember, relationships are about compromise. You have to find something that you both want to do. Don't give into friends who always want you to do what they want.

3 Give a compliment
Everyone loves an ego boost. Noticing something you like about someone and sharing it with him or her is a great way to start a conversation.

4 Turn off the technology!
If you're constantly checking your voicemail, text messages or listening to an MP3 player you give other people the message that you're unavailable or uninterested in them.

1 💬 **Work in pairs. Read the webpage, then close your book and tell your partner what advice it offers.**

2 (1/58) **Listen to someone trying to make a date, then answer the questions.**

1 What does Dave do right, according to the advice on the webpage?

2 What errors does Dave commit, according to Samantha's tips?

3 💬 **You are going to ask someone out on a date. Choose who will be Student A and Student B.**

Student A

You are going to ask Student B out on a date. You should …

• ask about how he/she spends their free time.

• try to show a genuine interest in what you hear.

• use Samantha's tips to move the conversation on to the key question.

Invite Student B out on a date.

Student B

You are potentially interested in Student A as a partner for a date. However, your decision depends on whether he/she …

• shows genuine interest in you.

• has similar free-time interests to you.

• proposes something that sounds fun.

Remember to turn down student A if you are not satisfied!

Strategy

Using *just*

Read extracts 1 and 2 from the listening in 2. Match them to uses a and b.

1 I was just wondering, do you want to do something later?

a To indicate that something is inconvenient or impossible.

2 Well, it's just that I had something else planned.

b To mean 'only' or to indicate that something is optional.

Use *just* to help you indicate that an offer you make is optional and to decline an unwanted invitation.

Vocabulary

1 **From the list of activities in the Phrase bank find ...**

1 three team sports.

2 a winter sport and a water sport.

3 four activities you would do in a gym.

4 two activities you would do in a park.

2 **Write five words or expressions from the Phrase bank to describe this sequence of events**

start an activity – enrol on a course – learn without difficulty – continue trying – stop doing something

3 **Substitute the expressions in bold with percentages and the word *approximately*.**

Screen Time

Just under a third of teenagers have their own computer and **four out of ten** have their own camera. **Nearly half** of the students interviewed said they watched DVDs at least once a month, and **one in five** watches every week. **A little over three-quarters** of the respondents said they connected to the internet daily, and **almost all** of those we surveyed said they watched television every day.

Pronunciation

4 **Write the words under the correct headings.**

teenagers   students   DVDs   watches   three-quarters   respondents

/s/	/z/	/ɪz/

Functional language

5a **Make complete sentences to create a dialogue using the prompts below.**

Mike   you / free / Saturday night?

Anna   why?

Mike   wonder / fancy / go out / pizza?

Anna   mmm / not fancy / pizza

Mike   Chinese?

Anna   good idea

Mike   8 o'clock?

Anna   make / later?

Mike   8.30?

Anna   great / call/ you / then

5b (1/59) **Listen and check.**

6 **Work in pairs to practise the dialogue.**

Phrase bank

basketball
cycling   skiing
work out   aerobics
weight training
badminton
squash   swimming
hockey
martial arts
Pilates   spinning
yoga   darts   pool
tenpin bowling
running

take something up
pick something up
sign up for something
stick at something
give up something
take part in something

bar   court   track
pool   gym   pitch
mountains   park

Do you fancy ...
meeting up with ...?
going to the cinema?
going to a gig?
playing pool/snooker/
   darts?

Are you free on
   Saturday night?
I wondered if you
   wanted to go.
What's happening?
What's on?
Could we make it a
   little later?
Is there anything else?
I'll give you a call later.
We'll call for you
   around 7.
Oh yeah, nice one.
Great.
Mmm, maybe.
Well, I'll see.

 Now watch the DVD episode Free time

7

The hard sell

Phrase bank

brand name
commercials
logo
pop-up
slogan
classified ads
sponsorship

advertisement
consumer
promotion
products

Vocabulary: advertising

1 Label the photos with words from the Phrase bank.

The future's bright.

The future's Orange.

orange™
hutchison telecom

Orange, 2008

1. _____   2. _____   3. _____

2 Match words from the Phrase bank with definitions 1-4.

1 An online advert that suddenly appears when your cursor moves over part of a website
2 Small adverts in the final pages of a newspaper
3 A group of adverts that are broadcast between scheduled programmes
4 The name of a company that sells or markets a product

Culture

The first TV commercial was shown in the USA in 1941 and cost $4. Since then *commercial breaks* or *the ads* have become a part of TV channels everywhere.

3 Find synonyms in the Phrase bank for the words below.

buyer _____   commercial _____
goods _____   selling _____

4 Read the article about how advertising works, then match a word in bold to the definitions.

Global Games announced the **launch** of its latest product for the teenage **market** today: an interactive computer game. To promote their product, the company contracted an **advertising agency** to plan a 12-month **campaign** of advertisements on **hoardings** in every major city, thousands of **posters** at bus stops and millions of **flyers** to be given out to teenagers.

1 a company whose work is to design the promotion of products _____
2 a group of actions designed to promote a product _____
3 large advertisements often seen at the side of a busy road _____
4 medium-sized, paper-based advertisements _____
5 a group of people who might want to buy something _____
6 printed adverts given directly to members of the public _____
7 the start of the promotion of a new product _____

Language note

The musical theme or short song that accompanies many ads or announcements on TV and radio is called a *jingle*.

5 Complete this table of word families.

verb	noun (person)	noun (thing)
consume	consumer	_____
_____	_____	advertisement
_____	promoter	_____
_____	_____	production
sponsor	_____	

Speaking: discussing adverts

1 🔘1/60 **Read 1-5 below then listen to five conversations. Number the descriptions in the order in which you hear them.**

1 Two people discussing a promotion on a web page. ___

2 Two people talking about a TV advertisement. ___

3 A group of people who work in an advertising agency. ___

4 A commercial for a health supplement. ___

5 A university lecture on advertising. ___

2 🔘1/60 **Listen again and answer the questions.**

1 Can you complete the slogan, 'Designed by artists, built by robots, _____'

2 What's the name of the health product? _____

3 What needs to be done to improve the jingle? _____

4 What is the most important characteristic of a good logo? _____

5 What two types of advertising from page 40 is the agency going to use?
_____

3 **Write synonyms from the Phrase bank for each of the criteria for a good advert. A good advert ...**

1 communicates a message.

2 has music or a song that sticks in the memory.

3 persuades existing customers to continue using the product.

4 causes a strong effect on customers.

5 familiarizes people with a product.

4 🗩 **Work with a partner. Complete the sentences below using your own ideas. Work in pairs to practise the dialogue.**

A Have you seen that new _____ advert?

B Which one?

A The one with the _____ – I think it's really cool.

B Oh yeah, the one with the slogan '_____'

Phrase bank

makes an impact
gets an idea across
is catchy
raises brand
   awareness
encourages brand
   loyalty

Culture

Since it began in 1922, the BBC has never broadcast any *ad breaks*.

Language note

Publicity is the interest or attention that people give to a thing, person or event.

He attracted a lot of bad publicity after the newspaper scandal.

Advertising is the business of trying to persuade people to buy products or services.

They launched an important advertising campaign.

Pronunciation

/əʊ/ **and** /ɒ/ **sounds**

a 🔘1/61 **Listen to the words and note the** /əʊ/ **and** /ɒ/ **sounds.**

zone   song

b **Say the words. Underline the** /əʊ/ **or** /ɒ/ **sound.**

radio   slogan   logo
login   pop-up   poster

c 🔘1/62 **Listen and check.**

Listening: advertising and health

1 Read quotations 1 and 2 from the book *Fast Food Nation*. Match them to A and B below.

1 'Children spend about seven hours a day, 150 days a year in school. Those hours have in the past been largely free of advertising.'

2 'Eight-year-olds are considered ideal customers; they have about 65 years of purchasing ahead of them.'

A a potential opportunity
B a wasted opportunity

2 What do you think the listening is going to be about?

a diet in modern society
b what children do at school
c the frustrations of marketing executives
d the financing of education in the US

3 🔊 1/63 Listen to the radio programme. Check your answer to 2 then decide if the statements below are true or false. Correct the false sentences.

1 The listening explains how advertising became a part of US school life as a way of increasing choice for school children. ___

2 Parents were involved in the negotiations with advertisers. ___

3 The adverts were shown on school buses, in sports grounds and in the school. ___

4 A large percentage of advertising in schools is for junk food. ___

5 Critics worry that the advertising campaigns could have dangerous long-term consequences for students. ___

4 Work in pairs to answer the questions, then check your answers with another pair.

1 In what ways could the campaign be considered positive?
2 What are the two main arguments against the scheme?
3 Does anything similar happen in your country?

5 💬 Do you think advertising in schools is a good idea? Discuss in pairs. Use the Language note to help you.

THE INTERNATIONAL BESTSELLER

'A shocking exposé ... could make a difference to the way we eat. For ever.'
Evening Standard

FAST FOOD NATION

ERIC SCHLOSSER

What the All-American Meal is Doing to the World

Functional language: pros and cons

1 **Read the words and expressions in the Phrase bank.**
Find examples to complete post-it notes 1-3.

1
two phrases used in the opening sentence of the discussion to indicate that there are different opinions
_____
_____

2
four phrases used to talk about the positive aspects of the scheme
_____
_____

3
four phrases used to talk about problems associated with the scheme
_____
_____
_____

2 **Listen to a speech discussing the pros and cons of product placement advertising. Answer the questions.**

1 What are the arguments in favour of product placement (the pros)?
2 What are the arguments against product placement (the cons)?
3 What is the speaker's opinion?

3 💬 **Work in pairs to discuss the task. Use the phrases in 1 and your own ideas to write a speech about the pros and cons of the proposal.**

> **Task**   There is too much advertising of violent toys in the media. Adverts for these toys should be banned. Discuss.

4 1/65 **Listen to someone giving a speech about banning the advertising of violent toys to children. Does your opinion coincide with the speaker's? Why/why not?**

Pronunciation 🔵

Sentence stress

a **Read the opening sentence of a speech. Which words do you think will be stressed? Remember to look for the key words in the sentence.**

One of the most subtle forms of modern advertising is product placement in films.

b 1/66 **Listen and practise saying the line, using the same pronunciation.**

Final task: giving a speech

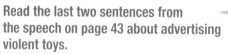

Watch for cars when wearing headphones

NSW Police Force
www.police.nsw.gov.au

1 **Look at the poster and answer the questions.**

1 What message do you think the poster is trying to get across?

2 Who do you think it is directed at?

3 Did this image make an impact on you?

2 (1/67) **Listen to a student's speech about the task below. How could it have been better?**

3 **Think of an opening line for your speech that will clarify the subject. Think of a closing line that will leave the listener thinking.**

Strategy

Read the last two sentences from the speech on page 43 about advertising violent toys.

Should children be free to watch whatever they want? Most of us would agree that they should not.

This type of rhetorical question is a common way to finish a speech or presentation. Why do you think the answer to the question is given in its full rather than its contracted ('they shouldn't') form?

Task **You are going to give a speech on the proposal:**

Governments should use the power of advertising and shocking images to change the behaviour of young people.

Remember to …

• give the arguments for and against the proposal.

• include an opening sentence.

• write a good opening sentence using key words for argument.

• use a rhetorical sentence to close your speech.

• give your speech without reading directly from your notes.

• stress the key words and arguments in your speech.

4 💬 **Write a speech on the subject. Include functional expressions from page 43.**

Vocabulary

1 **Find the odd one out and explain why.**

1 a hoarding, a jingle, a poster _____

2 an advertiser, a sponsor, a consumer _____

3 a slogan, a classified ad, a pop-up _____

2 **Write the verb forms of each noun. Mark the stressed syllables for the nouns and the verbs.**

1 product _____

2 consumer _____

3 advertising _____

4 sponsorship _____

5 promoter _____

3 1/68 **Listen to the definitions and choose the correct word from the list.**

consumer   flyer   jingle   launch   logo   own-brand   slogan

Definition 1 _____

Definition 2 _____

Definition 3 _____

Definition 4 _____

Definition 5 _____

Pronunciation

4 **Write the /əʊ/ or /ɒ/ symbol next to words 1-5 below according to their pronunciation.**

1 opponents

2 poster

3 pros

4 cons

5 open

Functional language

5 **Write words from the Phrase bank for each of the definitions 1-3.**

1 People who don't like something

2 People who do like an idea

3 Something that is liked by some and disliked by others.

6 **Work in pairs. Choose a topic. You have one minute to think of the pros and cons. Then give a speech to your partner on the topic, using the expressions from the Phrase bank.**

wearing school uniform

using a bicycle to travel in your city

finishing the school day at 2.30

spreading holidays more evenly through the year instead of having a long summer holiday

Phrase bank

brand name
banner
logo pop-up
slogan
classified ad
sponsorship

consumer
advertisement
products
promotion

makes an impact
gets an idea across
is catchy
raises brand
    awareness
encourages brand
    loyalty

fast food
junk food
controversial
devastating
exposed to
directed at
exploiting

... has been a focus
    for argument and
    controversy for
    some time
Those in favour of
    the project ...
Critics argue that ...
Supporters of the
    scheme say ...
But a more major area
    of concern is ...
The benefits are
    obvious
But opponents point
    out that ...
One of the most
    controversial
    innovations in
    recent years was ...
There are very real
    fears that ...
There's no doubt
    that facilities have
    improved

8 Studying

Vocabulary: assessment

A. B. C. D.

1 **Look at the pictures. Use words from the Phrase bank to describe the people.**

2 **Match nouns from the Phrase bank to the definitions.**

1 a repeat exam for a subject you failed _____

2 the grade you get by adding all your marks and dividing by the number of assignments you did _____

3 system of evaluation over time, not based on exams _____

4 a practice exam you do before an official exam _____

5 studying in preparation for exams _____

6 the marks you get for an exam or a piece of work _____

7 work you do at home or at school _____

3 **2/01 Use words from 2 to complete the text. Listen and check.**

Qualifications in Britain used to depend completely on exam performance, but now more courses are assessed on a mix of (1) _____, done over time, and exams. In some subjects, up to 40% of the final mark comes from (2) _____ of assignments. Students who get nervous doing exams have welcomed this change, because they feel that their (3) _____ is better than their exam results.

A levels are very important for getting into further education, so it's common for schools to have (4) _____ in January to give students a chance to practise before they do the real thing in June. No-one wants to do (5) _____, and many universities require specific A level (6) _____ to get onto a course, so many students spend much of May and early June doing (7) _____.

4 **Answer the questions.**

1 How important is continuous assessment in your school?

2 Does your school have mock exams?

3 Do you prefer to be evaluated by coursework or by exams?

4 Do you study through the term, or leave it to last-minute revision?

Speaking: talking about progress

1 Complete the definitions with words from the Phrase bank.

1 A _____ is a reduced version of a text written in your own words.

2 An _____ is a piece of work you do at home and then give in to your teacher.

3 If you copy another person's work without adding your own ideas to it, you _____ it. This is common when students copy texts from the internet, but beware, many teachers have programs to check on this.

4 To make revising for exams easier, students should regularly _____ their notes throughout the year.

5 _____ is what students do when they write down the main points of a spoken presentation as they listen to it.

6 When you search for information in an organized way on the internet or in a library, you _____ a subject.

2 2/02 You're going to listen to a student talking about how different sixth form is. Which things will she mention? Listen and check.

uniform	timetables	classes	homework assignments
problems of internet research		frequency of exams	
balance of exams and coursework			

3 2/02 Listen again. Complete part of the dialogue using words from the Pronunciation box.

Interviewer So how are things different now (1) _____ a sixth former?

Student Well, of course the difference most people notice first is that we don't have to (2) _____ uniform.

Interviewer Yes, I (3) _____ that's pretty popular.

Student That's (4) _____, and (5) _____ timetable is more flexible. But I think there are also (6) _____ important differences when it comes to the type of work we do.

4 ▶ In pairs, ask each other about differences between secondary school and what you're studying now. Use the conversation in 3 to help you.

Phrase bank

note-taking
summary
assignment
research
plagiarize
review

working independently
flexible

Culture

In the USA, the equivalent of A levels is called Advanced Placement or Standard Assessment Test.

Pronunciation

Homophones

a 2/03 Listen to the words. Write another word with a different spelling but the same pronunciation.

some _____
our _____
hear _____
you're _*your*_
wear _____
right _____

Phrase bank

detailed notes
bullet points
mind map
colour-coded
  notes

optional activities
note-taking
visual learners

Useful language

I think 3 is more useful than …

While 4 is a useful skill, … is something you need to do more often.

OK, let's discard this one because …

Listening: study skills

1 💬 **Work with a partner. Read study skills 1-6. Which three are most important? Use the Useful language to discuss.**

1 a good variety of IT skills
2 organizing your time
3 effective reading
4 using the internet critically
5 ability to plan and write good essays
6 good note-taking

2 2/04 **Listen to a Head Teacher giving a start of term lecture to new sixth formers. Which three things from 1 does she mention?**

3 **Match expressions 1-5 to meanings a-e. What do they all have in common?**

1 a busy social life
2 at the last minute
3 meet a deadline
4 on a regular basis
5 part time

a the latest possible time for doing something
b something that you do routinely
c a full free-time agenda
d for a few hours each day or week
e a specific time or date, a time limit

4 **Look at the different study techniques and label them using words from the Phrase bank.**

1. _____

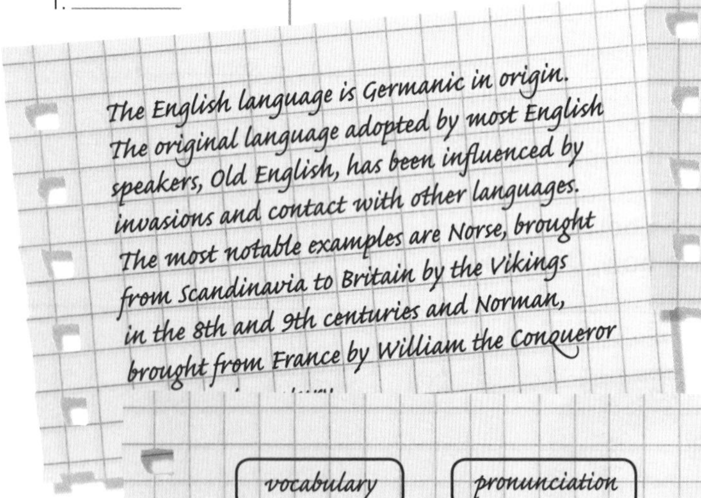

The English language is Germanic in origin. The original language adopted by most English speakers, Old English, has been influenced by invasions and contact with other languages. The most notable examples are Norse, brought from Scandinavia to Britain by the Vikings in the 8th and 9th centuries and Norman, brought from France by William the Conqueror ……

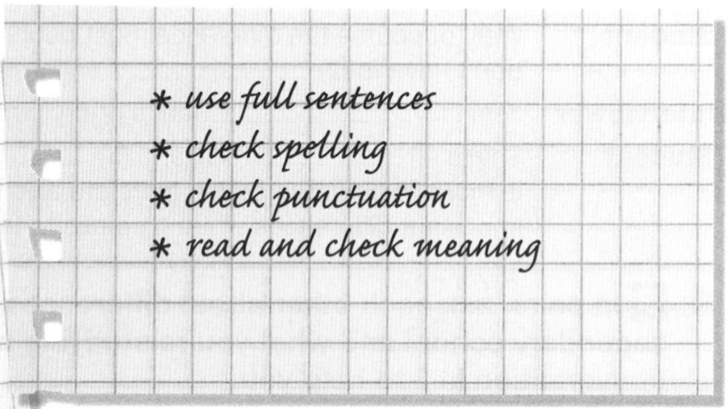

* use full sentences
* check spelling
* check punctuation
* read and check meaning

2. _____

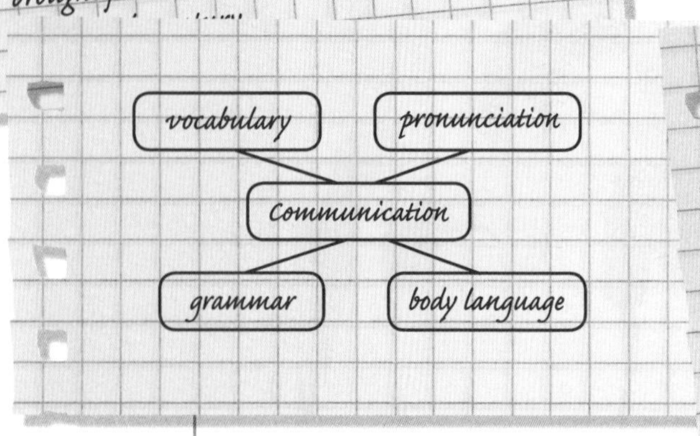

Some people write detailed notes using full sentences. Others note key words or write the most important information using bullet points. More visual learners may prefer to use mind maps or to colour-code their notes.

[mind map diagram: vocabulary — pronunciation — Communication — grammar — body language]

3. _____

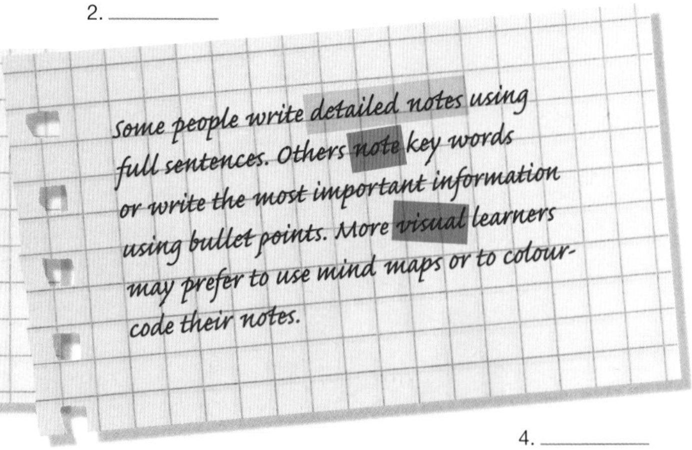

4. _____

5 2/05 **Listen to the presentation. Which technique in 4 is not mentioned?**

6 **Which of these have you tried? Which works best for you?**

Functional language: public speaking

1 **Find and write examples from the audioscript on page 104 of ways in which the speaker ...**

1 justifies why she is talking to the audience.

2 uses rhetorical questions to check understanding of important ideas.

3 uses imperatives to illustrate examples of desirable action.

4 uses the phrase 'It's easy ...' to introduce a problem.

5 uses words like 'some' and 'others' to talk about people's preferences.

2 **Use the Phrase bank to complete a speaker's presentation about essay writing.**

Writing essays is an important skill in sixth form and at university and (1) _____ to offer some tips about how to do this.

(2) _____ you need to do is thorough research. Read and use the internet, but don't forget to include your own ideas too. (3) _____ to spend so much time researching that we forget to think, so make sure you leave time to do this. (4) _____ is to plan: think what will come in each section of your essay and how best to organize it. (5) _____ it's important to start and finish well, so think about your introduction and try to finish with a strong conclusion. Try to support your ideas with quotations – (6) _____ – but please (7) _____ to include the name of the author and book that it comes from. (8) _____, leave yourself time to check your work. You don't want to ruin a good impression with silly spelling mistakes. (9) _____ can make all the difference between a mediocre essay and a great one.

Phrase bank

... you all know what I mean by that, don't you?
... don't forget
Following these simple tips
It's easy
... I'm here today
Remember
And finally
The first thing
The next thing

Language note

Easily confused words

Speakers give presentations to an audience.

~~Speakers give presentations to a public.~~

Pronunciation

/ə/

a 2/06 **Read and listen to the sentences. Note the /ə/ sound?**

I'm here to help you study better.

You'll have to think fast and work hard.

Try not to worry too much.

You have chosen to do a difficult subject.

It's easy to forget the simplest things.

b 2/06 **Listen again and practise pronouncing the /ə/ sound in 'to'.**

Final task: giving a presentation

1 **Read the strategy box. Listen to the two speakers. Which one uses the ideas in the strategy?**

2 **Read the index cards. Write a presentation about one of the skills. Use expressions from page 49.**

Speed reading

* reasons why we need to read quickly (research, amount of material ...)
* be clear about the info you want before you start, use contents, visual clues
* focus on main ideas, don't worry about descriptive detail
* don't move lips - slower reading
* practise - faster reading

1. _____

successful revision

* the right place and time - reduce distractions
* plan - importance of revision timetable
* condense your notes - gradually reduce down to postcard size
* record your notes - MP3
* plenty of food and sleep

2. _____

Presenting a project in class

* prepare well, research
* use visuals, Powerpoint, other resources
* involve the audience, time for questions
* practise it, don't read from notes
* keep calm, speak slowly

3. _____

Vocabulary

1 Explain the difference between these pairs of words

1 continuous assessment / exams
2 review / revision
3 detailed notes / bullet points
4 exam / mock exam
5 grade / average mark

2 Write words from the Phrase bank for definitions 1-4.

1 an essay or piece of work for your teacher _____
2 to do an exam again after you have failed it _____
3 to copy someone else's written work and say it is your own _____
4 summarizing the content of a presentation while listening _____

3 Complete the sentences with the correct form of a word from the Phrase bank.

1 If you copy another student's work you are _____ it.
2 _____ is a useful thing to do while your teacher is explaining things in class, that way you don't forget it.
3 Our teacher has _____ us three essays to do this week!
4 I like doing school projects because you get lots of time to _____ them on the internet.
5 I find it difficult to reduce a lot of information to simple ideas, that's why I hate doing _____.
6 It's a good idea to _____ the contents of each unit of work in your book when you complete them.

Pronunciation

4 Identify the words which are homophones and write an alternative spelling for each one under the correct heading.

wood   cake   meat   fish   see   ate   eye   chair   passed
two   one   four   six   whose   yes   star   no   which

Homophone	Alternative spelling

Functional language

5 Write four examples of language commonly used in giving a presentation.

6 💬 Think of a sport or activity that you do. Work in pairs and give a short presentation on how to be good at this activity. Include language from the Phrase bank.

Phrase bank

attentive
dedicated
exhausted
jubilant
overwhelmed
relieved
stressed
continuous assessment
mock exam
coursework
grades
average mark
re-take
revision

note-taking
summary
assignment
research
plagiarize
review

detailed notes
bullet points
index cards
mind map
successful revision
speed reading
presenting a project
   in class

You all know what I
   mean by that, don't
   you?
Don't forget
Following these simple
   tips
It's easy
I'm here today
Remember
And finally
The first thing
The next thing

Getting around

Phrase bank

bus lane
traffic jam
pedestrianized area
subway
zebra crossing
highway code
full driving licence
provisional driving
   licence
fine
parking ticket
traffic warden

Vocabulary: on the road

1. _____
2. _____
3. _____
4. _____
5. _____
6. _____

1 Label the photos with the words and phrases below.

give way   cycle lane   no entry   one way street
roundabout   traffic lights

Culture

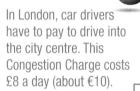

In London, car drivers have to pay to drive into the city centre. This Congestion Charge costs £8 a day (about €10).

2 Match the definitions to words from the Phrase bank.

1   a subterranean walkway _____

2   road congestion _____

3   a motorized vehicle-free zone _____

4   a section of the road for use by public transport only _____

5   a place for pedestrians to cross the road in safety _____

3 Complete the text with words from the Phrase bank.

Advice for road users travelling to Britain

The regulations for road users in the UK are called the (1) _____.

British teenagers can apply for a (2) _____ to drive a car under adult supervision when they are 17. However, they won't qualify for a (3) _____ unless they pass the theoretical and practical parts of a driving test.

Parking in the UK is strictly controlled. Prohibited areas are marked with a double yellow line. If you park in these areas you could get a (4) _____.

Bicycle users should also be aware that cycling on the pavement is prohibited. If the police see you doing this you could get a (5) _____.

Language note

pavement   sidewalk

4 Complete the transport collocations with words from the box.

lessons	test	licence	learner	dangerous	fully-qualified

*   _____ driver
*   _____ driver
*   _____ driver
*   driving _____
*   driving _____
*   driving _____

Speaking: comparing rules

1 **2/08** **Listen to a reporter asking a young woman in Madrid about government plans for changing driving regulations.**

2 **Complete her answer with the correct form of the words in brackets. Choose the correct alternatives in bold.**

I _____ (think) we need to learn to drive at 17. I _____ (live) in the city and public transport is **great/poor** so I _____ (be) in a rush to learn to drive. I think if people of my age could drive, there _____ (be) **more/fewer** accidents than now.

3 **2/09** **Listen to the radio programme and choose the best answer.**

1 The rules for driving in Spain and Britain are similar in the sense that …
  a the age when you can learn to drive is the same.
  b the parts of the test are the same.
  c the person who teaches learners is the same.
  d there are traffic accidents in both countries.

2 In Britain you can learn with …
  a a driving instructor.
  b anyone over the age of 21.
  c any qualified driver over the age of 21.
  d your relatives.

3 Under the new Spanish plan …
  a people can start learning to drive at a younger age.
  b people can learn to drive with anyone.
  c people can take the practical test before they are 18.
  d driving will be safer.

4 **Read the sentences. Do you agree (A) or disagree (D) with them? Write A or D.**

1 I don't think teenagers are responsible enough to drive.
2 I want to get my driving licence as soon as I'm 18.
3 They should teach everyone to drive in the sixth form at school.

5 **In pairs, ask each other about when young people should learn to drive. Use the woman's response in 2 to help you.**

Phrase bank

right-hand drive
confident drivers
dangerous drivers
driving instructor
speed limit
jump the lights
road rage

Culture

The 'L-plate' is an international sign for learner drivers. It began in the UK in 1935.

Once you have a British driving licence, you don't have to renew it until you are 70.

Pronunciation

-ed endings

a **2/10** **Listen and count the number of syllables in each pair of words.**

decide/decided   qualify/qualified
pass/passed   interest/interested

Past tense verbs ending in an /ɪd/ sound have one more syllable than the infinitive.

b **2/11** **Listen and write the words under the appropriate headings.**

started   played   bored
visited   frightened   studied
excited   learned

same number of syllables as infinitive	extra final syllable
studied	

tourist destination
spa
hot spring
Romans
architecture
museums
galleries
directing
tourist information
   office

Listening: understanding directions

1 🔘 2/12 **Read the map then listen and label the photos of places in Bath.**

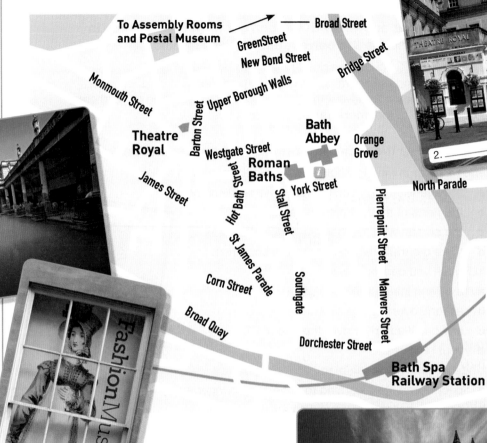

To Assembly Rooms
and Postal Museum

Broad Street

GreenStreet

New Bond Street

Bridge Street

Monmouth Street

Upper Borough Walls

Barton Street

Theatre Royal

Westgate Street

Bath Abbey

Orange Grove

Roman Baths

Hot Bath Street

York Street

James Street

Stall Street

St James Parade

North Parade

Pierrepoint Street

Manvers Street

Corn Street

Southgate

Broad Quay

Dorchester Street

Bath Spa Railway Station

1. _____

2. _____

FashionMuseum

3. _____

4. _____

Culture

Bath, a city in the south-west of England, is a UNESCO World Heritage Site.

Bath

2 🔘 2/12 **Listen again and answer the questions.**

1 How many people live in Bath?
2 Who built the first spa or hot spring baths there?
3 Where can you find these baths today?
4 What are the Assembly Rooms famous for now?
5 What is significant about the characters in Jane Austen's novels?
6 Why was 1987 an important year for Bath?

3 🔘 2/13 **Listen to the tourist officer at Bath train station giving directions. Look at the map to decide which of the city's attractions the tourists are visiting.**

1 Visitor 1 _____
2 Visitor 2 _____
3 Visitor 3 _____

Functional language: directions

1 Read the examples of types of expression normally used for giving directions.

imperatives	*Leave the station, take the second left*
imperatives + preposition of movement	*Go straight ahead, follow the road round to the right*
expressions to describe locations	*You'll see the river on your right, it's right opposite you*

2 Write two more examples from the Phrase bank for each category in 1.

3 Complete the tourist officer's directions with the words below.

across
on your right
take the first right
go straight up
the road round
turn left

Visitor	Hi, I want to get to the Postal Museum.
Tourist officer	OK, well you need to _____ out of the station and then _____ into Southgate.
Visitor	First left into South ...
Tourist officer	No, first right. OK, then you _____ Stall Street.
Visitor	Store Street?
Tourist officer	No, Stall Street – S-T-A-L-L.
Visitor	OK, Stall Street.
Tourist officer	Go straight ahead, _____ Westgate Street and Upper Borough Walls until you come to New Bond Street, where you turn left and follow _____.
Visitor	Sorry, New ...?
Tourist officer	New Bond Street. Turn left and follow the road round and then take the first right into Green Street. The museum's _____ on the corner with Broad Street.
Visitor	OK, terrific, thanks.

4 ⊙ 2/14 Listen and check. Pay attention to the corrective stress.

5 🗩 You are going to practise giving information and correcting errors. Read the task boxes and take turns to complete the activities.

Student A
Turn to page 105.
Follow the instructions.

Student B
Turn to page 106.
Follow the instructions.

Turn to page 105. Turn to page 106.

Phrase bank

Carry on straight across
When you get to the bridge
Turn left
Take the second left
You'll see the river on your right
Go straight ahead
It's on the corner to your left
That brings you to
Go up Southgate
Leave the station
Follow the road round to the right
Go straight up Manvers Street
Keep straight on into Stall Street
You'll see a big junction on your right
It's right opposite you

Pronunciation

Corrective stress

a 2/15 Listen to how we correct errors in understanding. This is called corrective stress.

No, first right.

No, Stall Street.

New Bond Street.

b 2/15 Listen again and repeat.

Final task: giving directions

1 (2/16) Read the strategy then listen to speakers A and B asking for directions. Which speaker uses a simpler style?

2 Order the words to make two simple requests for directions. Which speakers in 1 could have used these questions?

the / tell / airport / Hi / you / can / way/ fastest / to / me / the / ?

_____

the / please / station / Is / way / this / train / the / to / ?

_____

Strategy

In natural conversation, it's often unnecessary to use complex sentences. Use intonation and words like 'hi', 'excuse me' and 'please' to sound polite and friendly.

3 💬 Work in pairs. Decide who is Student A and Student B. Study the map of Madrid, then read the task boxes below.

Student A
1 You are in the Prado museum. Ask Student B for directions to the Puerta del Sol.
2 You are in the Thyssen museum. Ask Student B for directions to the Retiro Park.

Student B
1 You are in the Prado museum. Listen to Student A then give him/her directions.
2 You are in the Thyssen museum. Listen to Student A then give him/her directions.

Remember, Student A is a foreigner. Make sure you:
• use expressions to describe a location
• use imperatives so that the directions are clear.

4 Think of places that are within walking distance of your school. Write one place for 1–5 below.

1 somewhere you can do sports

_____

2 a public transport stop (eg, a metro station)

_____

3 a specialist shop (eg, a music shop)

_____

4 another school

_____

5 a place to go out in the evening

_____

5 💬 Swap your answers for 1-5 above. Take turns to ask for directions to each place.

Vocabulary

1 Correct the underlined words to make the sentences logical.

1 A <u>traffic warden</u> teaches you to drive.

2 You should never jump the <u>subway</u>.

3 A <u>speed limit</u> is a place where only buses can travel.

4 When you pass your driving test you are given a <u>provisional driving licence</u>.

5 You may get a <u>cycle lane</u> if you cycle on the pavement in the UK.

2 Use the expressions in the box to complete the text. You may need to change the form of the verbs.

| take the practical test   have driving lessons   full driving licence   theory test |

I **started** (1) _____ when I was seventeen and a half. The (2) _____ was quite easy because you can study that on the computer, and I **passed** that first time, but I found the practical part much more difficult. I (3) _____ for the first time just after my 18th birthday and – I **failed**. After that, though, my dad **helped** by taking me out to practise. I was pretty scared at first, but the extra practice made me feel more confident and when I took the test again last month, I passed. I was **delighted**! I received my (4) _____ this morning, so drivers beware!

Pronunciation

3 Say the words in bold in 2. How many syllables do they have?

4 Write the words in bold under the correct heading.

/t/ /d/	/ɪd/

Functional language

5 Put the sentences in the correct order in this dialogue.

Visitor	Morning. I'm looking for the City Cinema Complex. _1_
Visitor	Brightwell Street? ___
Visitor	Great, thanks very much. ___
Visitor	Is there anywhere to park? ___
Visitor	OK, and then what? ___
Visitor	Sorry, was that the third on the left or the right? ___
Tourist officer	No, Brighton Street. ___
Tourist officer	No problem. ___
Tourist officer	OK, well you need to go out of here and turn right, and then carry on down the road till you get to Brighton Street. ___
Tourist officer	The left. Go straight down Goodall Avenue to the end, and it's right opposite. ___
Tourist officer	Turn right into Brighton Street, and then you need the second, no, third street on the left – I think it's called Goodall Avenue. ___
Tourist officer	Yes, there's a big car park on the far side of the cinema. ___

6 **Choose two places in your city. Give directions to your partner. Can they guess which places you chose?**

Phrase bank

bus lane
traffic jam
pedestrianized area
subway   fine
zebra crossing
highway code
full driving licence
provisional driving
  licence
parking ticket
traffic warden

right-hand drive
confident drivers
dangerous drivers
driving instructor
speed limit
jump the lights
road rage

tourist destination
spa   hot spring
architecture
museums
galleries
directing
tourist information
  office

Turn left
Go straight ahead
Leave the station
Keep straight on into
  Stall Street
Take the second left
Go up Southgate
Carry on straight
  across
Go straight up Manvers
  Street
That brings you to
When you get to the
  bridge
It's right opposite you
You'll see the river on
  your right
You'll see a big junction
  on your right
Follow the road round
  to the right
It's on the corner to
  your left

Now watch the DVD episode Transport

Prepare to ...
describe a photo

A

1 In pairs, look at the photos then read the words below. Write A or B to indicate which photo you associate with each word.

chubby cheeks ___   wrinkles ___   twinkling brown eyes ___
curly blond hair ___   laughter lines ___

2 Read the words for describing physical appearance. Write them under the appropriate headings.

a bit overweight   a mole   a piercing   middle-aged
shoulder-length   balding   a scar   in her teens   cropped
curvy   freckles   a toddler   elderly   in his late twenties
a tattoo   slim   straight   wavy   well-built

hair features	build	age	distinguishing features
			a scar

3 ▭ Work in pairs. Student A describes someone in the class. Student B tries to guess who it is.

4 🔊 2/17 Listen to a description of the people in photos A and B. Tick the things the speaker does.

- describes what the people look like ☐
- talks about what they're wearing ☐
- tries to guess how old the people are ☐
- tries to guess how they're feeling ☐
- tries to guess something about their character ☐

B

Remember: Unit 5

a In Unit 5, you prepared to describe photos of places. Write any expressions you can remember for ...

describing a photo
speculating about what is in the photo
giving an opinion

b Check your answers on page 29.

5 **2/17** **Listen again to the speaker in 4 and complete the sentences.**

1 There's an important difference between them and that's ...

2 You can tell she's old because ...

3 The woman is with other people, but the baby is ...

4 I don't think he's Spanish – he could be from somewhere ...

6 **Which sentences in 5 ...**

1 describes either A or B? ___

2 contrasts both photos? ___

Useful language **A-Z**

Describing age:

He's around 17.
He's in his early/
    mid/late 20s/40s.
She's 60ish.

7 **Read the phrases used to compare and contrast photos. Match the beginnings to an appropriate ending.**

1 In the first picture we can see X ...

2 The photo on top is of X ...

3 Both pictures ...

4 In both ...

5 They're quite similar in that ... However, ...

a an important difference is ...

b whereas the photo at the bottom ...

c are photos of people

d cases we can see ...

e whereas in the second ...

8 **Complete the sentences in 7 to make comparisons of the photos on page 58.**

9 💬 **In pairs, take turns to describe two photos. Decide who is Student A and Student B, then do the task.**

Task

Student A

You are going to describe the photos on this page.

Compare and contrast the photos. Describe what you can see and how you think the people are feeling.

Student B

You are going to describe the photos on page 105.

Compare and contrast the photos. Describe what you can see and how you think the people are feeling.

1

2

Prepare to...
talk about a proposal

1 **Read the words for describing fame and success. Write them under the appropriate headings.**

bestseller   blockbuster   ~~celebrity~~   fan   gold medallist   star
hit series   one-hit wonder   platinum album   gossip column
paparazzi   autograph hunter   notorious   famous   award-winning

people	things you can read	films and tv	music	adjectives
celebrity				

2 **Answer the questions about the words in 1.**

1 Which word means 'famous person'?
2 Which word means 'admirer of famous person'?
3 Which word means 'popular book'?
4 Which of the music expressions describes a band with limited success?
5 Which expression could you use to describe Lost or CSI?

3 **Write an example from your country for each of the following.**

1 a hit series
2 a bestseller
3 a platinum album
4 a gold medallist
5 a celebrity

4 **2/18 Listen to someone talking about the effects of celebrity on society. The speaker makes a number of points. Which option, A, B or C, best summarizes these?**

A

Negative effect
Negative effect
Negative effect
Negative effect
Negative effect
Negative effect
Conclusion

B

Negative effect
Negative effect
Negative effect
Positive effect
Positive effect
Positive effect
Conclusion

C

Negative effect
Positive effect
Positive effect
Negative effect
Negative effect
Positive effect
Conclusion

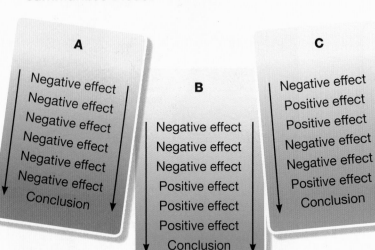

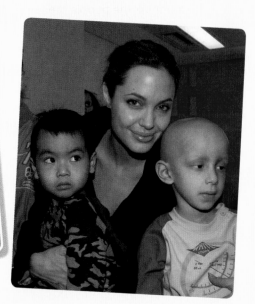

5 Read points 1-6 below then listen to the speaker in 4 again. Number the points in the order in which she mentions them.

1 a good example to the young ___

2 fame without effort ___

3 a source of pleasure ___

4 an unrealistic goal ___

5 a decline in quality of TV and magazines ___

6 using your fame to help other people ___

6 Do you agree with the speaker's arguments?

7 Read the connectors in the table. Write a heading for each column of the table using the phrases in blue below.

to conclude your argument   to contrast points   to add points

It also seems that ... Another consequence is ... Another thing we mustn't forget is ... On top of this ...	However, on a more positive note ... On the other hand ... But at the same time ...	To sum up ... At the end of the day ... All in all ...

8 💬 In pairs, prepare a speech about the pros and cos of the proposal in the Task box. Decide who is Student A and Student B, then complete the task.

Task

TV talent shows should be banned. Discuss.

Student A

Prepare a speech about the proposal above. When you're ready, give your speech.

Student B

Listen to Student A's speech. Check if he/she ...

• gives arguments for and against the proposal

• uses examples

• uses connectors

Prepare to...
do a project

1 Look at the photos of people campaigning to change society. What do you think they want to do?

STOP KNIVES
SAVE LIVES

2 (2/19) Listen to two people talking about a TV programme about campaigners for social change called Battlefront. Choose the best answer.

1 The project started ...
a on TV.
b in schools.
c on the internet.
d in London.

2 The programme included projects by ...
a 20 people.
b 22 people.
c 200 people.
d 12 people.

3 The objective was to ...
a raise money.
b get the government to change things.
c have fun.
d get people to change.

4 One campaigner wanted ...
a to ban smoking.
b to stop people using mp3 players.
c to reduce road accidents.
d to ban cars.

5 The Londoner wanted to ...
a stop modelling.
b reduce violent street crime.
c talk about his friend.
d be famous.

6 The campaigners had to ...
a wear special T-shirts.
b use a variety of techniques.
c make a film.
d talk to politicians.

3 In pairs, discuss your answers to the following questions.

1 If you want to change something in your country, how can you do it?
2 Why do you think the programme is called Battlefront?
3 Do you think individuals can make a difference?

Project

Design a campaign to raise awareness of an issue.
Your project must include ...

- a poster to advertise your campaign
- a catchy name for your campaign, a slogan and a logo
- what your project aims to change
- the people your project is aimed at
- suggestions for how to get media attention for your campaign.

4 **Read the project. Choose one of the following issues for your project or another subject you feel strongly about.**

sports facilities in your local area   cruelty to animals

young people's rights   education   junk food   violent crime

5 **Work in groups. Present your project to the class. Use the Useful language to help you.**

Remember: Unit 5

a **Write any expressions you can remember for ...**
making suggestions
agreeing and disagreeing
confirming your decisions

b **Check your answers on page 33.**

Useful language

Explaining your ideas, reasons and objectives

Our campaign is called ...
We thought this would be a good idea because ...
We believe this is a very important issue because ...
We think this will appeal to (who?) because ...
Our goal is to ...
Through this campaign we aim to ...

Talking about the different aspects of your plan

We plan to use a variety of techniques such as ...
Some of the different aspects of the campaign include ...
As well as X, we're going to ...
The campaign is in three phases: first ..., second ..., and finally ...
The campaign will start/ conclude with ...

11

Eating out

1. _____

2. _____

3. _____

cookies
curry
fresh orange juice
fish and chips
dark chocolate

balanced
exotic
healthy
processed
hot
locally-produced
rich
vegetarian

acidic
bitter
spicy
greasy
sickly

Vocabulary: food

1 Look at the photos and label them using words from the Phrase bank.

2 Read the adjectives in the box. Are they generally positive or negative? Use one to describe each of the foods in 1.

acidic	bitter	greasy	sickly	spicy

3 Read the words in the Phrase bank. Write ...

1 One antonym for each of words a–c ...
   a home-made _____
   b mild _____
   c low-fat _____
2 Two words that describe where food comes from
3 Three words that describe types of diet

4. _____

5. _____

4 Read the words in the box and translate them into your language.

dishes	healthy diet	food allergies	curry
sweet tooth	nuts	vegan diet	vegetarian

Culture

Very spicy dishes, like curry, are popular in Britain. If food is spicy, people describe it as 'hot' or 'chilli-hot' to distinguish the taste from the temperature.

5 Use the words in 4 to complete the text about food in Britain.

HOME	ENGLAND	SCOTLAND	WALES	N. IRELAND	FORUM

The traditional British dish was a simple 'meat and two veg'. Fortunately, tastes have changed. The British are now more aware of the need for a
(1) _____ and more people are choosing to give up meat and become
(2) _____. Others go further and try not to eat any dairy products, like cheese or eggs. This is called a (3) _____.

The British also enjoy a lot of foreign (4) _____. Britain's historical connections with India explain why we British like spicy food, especially
(5) _____.

British people are also famous for having a (6) _____. However, this fondness for cakes and biscuits may be related to increasing numbers of disorders like (7) _____ and diabetes. Intolerance to foods like
(8) _____ and gluten are now quite common.

Language Note

When we talk about food that is typical of a place we use the word *dish*.

~~A common Italian plate is spaghetti.~~

A common Italian dish is **spaghetti**.

Speaking: talking about food

1 **Read the questions. Think of one more question about food.**

1 Do you normally eat home-made or convenience food?
2 If you eat out with friends, where do you go?
3 Have you ever tried English food? What was it?
4 Do you know any vegetarians?

2 💬 **In pairs, ask and answer the questions in 1. Use the Phrase bank to help you.**

3 **Use words from the Phrase bank to complete the food collocations.**

cup _and saucer_   fish _____   salt _____
knife _____   bread _____   bacon _____
strawberries _____   bangers _____

4 🎧 2/20 **Listen and check. Pay attention to the pronunciation of 'and'.**

5 **Label the photos with the descriptions below.**

1 A foreign student in a host family.
2 Friends out for a meal.
3 A customer and waiter.

6 🎧 2/21 **Listen to the people's conversations. What is the problem in each conversation?**

A. _____

B. _____

C. _____

Phrase bank

fast food restaurant
takeaway food

too sweet
too bitter
too greasy
too spicy

...and saucer
...and pepper
...and fork
...and chips
...and butter
...and eggs
...and cream
...and mash

a bit heavy
a bit sickly

Culture

Two traditional British meals are:

steak and kidney pie with chips

bangers and mash (sausages with pureed potatoes)

Pronunciation

/dʒ/ and /g/ sounds

a 🎧 2/22 **Listen to the words. Which have the /dʒ/ sound and which have the /g/ sound?**

allergy   greasy
juice   vegan

b 🎧 2/23 **Read the words. Which have the /dʒ/ sound and which have the /g/ sound? Listen and check.**

vegetarian   gluten
burger   sausages

Phrase bank

bill
cheeseburger
eat in
drive through
fries
ketchup
regular
waiter
mustard
take out
starter
tip
fizzy drinks
main course

1 **Which of the words in the Phrase bank would you associate with...**

- a fast food restaurant
- a standard restaurant

2 **Read the sentences about the history of convenience foods. Try to guess the missing information.**

In the US in the mid-1950s, McDonald's only had one portion size for its french fries: that size was called (1) _____

Since then, portions have been getting bigger. Today's (2) _____ weighs the same as the 1998 (3) _____

The sizes of fast-food portions in Europe are (4) _____ than those in the United States.

An (5) _____ cola in London, Rome, and Dublin is only a (6) _____ in the US.

3 2/24 **Listen to the information in 2 and check your answers.**

4 2/25 **Read the menu. Listen and tick the items the customer orders.**

Language note

| chips | fries |
| biscuit | cookie |

In English, we mainly use the word *rations* to talk about a small or limited amount of something to eat or drink, e.g., *emergency rations.*

We use the words *portions* and *servings* to talk about the standardized quantities of food served in restaurants.

MENU
An Excellent choice!

burger	£1.99	regular fries	£0.99	chicken nuggets	£1.99
megaburger	£3.99	large fries	£1.49	cola – regular/large	£0.99 £1.49
chicken burger	£2.49	extra large fries	£1.99	diet cola – regular/large	£0.99 £1.49
bacon cheeseburger	£2.99	chicken wings	£2.99	orange – regular/large	£0.99 £1.49
chicken salad	£2.49	onion rings	£0.99	water	£0.99

5 2/25 **Listen again and decide if the statements are true or false.**

1 The customer wants to eat in. ___

2 The customer pays with a £20 note. ___

3 The customer asks for mustard. ___

4 Each person pays for their own food. ___

5 Before the meal, they played basketball. ___

Functional language: food orders

Phrase bank

checking the order
sharing out the food
giving an order to the
customer
offering to pay
ordering
refusing money

Culture

In English, the word *cheers* is traditionally used to toast or celebrate something, often with alcohol.

Today, we use the word to say thank you, especially when receiving food.

Language note

I'll get this.

It's on me.

My treat.

~~I want to invite you.~~

1 Read the groups of expressions in the table below. Write a heading for each one using words from the Phrase bank.

• I'd like two bacon cheeseburgers. • Actually, give us some onion rings. • Could I have some ketchup, please?	• Do you want any fries with that? • And to drink? • Would you like those drinks regular or large? • Anything else with that?	• Here you go. • Here you are.
• So that's a bacon cheeseburger for you. • And yours was a chicken sandwich with water.	• What do I owe you?	• My treat – you can pay another day.

2 Find synonyms in the table for the following phrases…

1 It's on me.
2 What would you like to drink?
3 How much does this cost?
4 Take your food, please.
5 Tomato sauce, please.
6 Would you like chips?

3 💬 Work in pairs. One of you works in a fast-food restaurant, the other is a customer. Take turns to make food orders.

Pronunciation

Consonant clusters

a 2/26 Read the words. Listen and repeat.

excuse me   breakfast
drinks   baked beans
actually   exactly

b 2/27 Read these words and practise saying them. Listen and check your pronunciation.

vegetables sandwich
oranges biscuits crisps

Final task: ordering food by phone

MARCO'S PIZZA
TAKE AWAY MENU

PIZZA	SMALL	REGULAR	FAMILY
Pepperoni	£3.99	£4.99	£5.99
Mediterranean	£4.49	£5.49	£6.49
Four seasons	£3.99	£4.99	£5.99
Four cheeses	£4.49	£5.49	£6.49
Seafood special	£4.99	£5.99	£6.99

Extra toppings 50p each:
mushrooms, olives, pepperoni, ham, cheese

Side orders:
green salad £1.49   garlic bread £1.49   chicken wings £1.99

Drinks:
cola 99p   lemonade 99p   orange juice 69p
apple juice 69p   sparkling water 99p

1 2/28 **Listen to two customers calling a pizza delivery company. Answer the questions.**

1 What did customer A say when she didn't understand?
2 What did customer B say when he didn't understand?
3 How did the pizza delivery person rephrase the question?

2  **Work in pairs. Choose your tasks and follow the instructions.**

Student A
You are a customer:
- Read the menu.
- Order a pizza. Read the telephone dialogue and complete it in a logical way.
- Prepare to respond to questions. Read the Strategy and memorize your responses.

Student B
You work for the pizza delivery company:
- Read the telephone dialogue and memorize your questions to the customer.
- Prepare to rephrase anything the customer doesn't understand.

Language note
 I beg your pardon.   Excuse me.

Strategy

Speaking by phone is easier if you can predict what the other person is going to say or ask. This gives you time to prepare responses.

a What response do these questions require?

1 Is that traditional or deep pan crust?

2 And is this for home delivery or to collect?

b If you don't understand a question, make this clear rather than guessing what was said.

Pizza man	Good evening, Marco's Pizza.
Customer	_____
Pizza man	And is this for home delivery or to collect?
Customer	_____
Pizza man	OK, what would you like to order?
Customer	_____
Pizza man	Is that traditional or deep pan crust?
Customer	_____
Pizza man	Regular or family size?
Customer	_____
Pizza man	And would you like any extra ingredients?
Customer	_____?
Pizza man	Mushrooms, olives, pepperoni, extra cheese ...
Customer	_____
Pizza man	Anything else?
Customer	_____
Pizza man	OK, that'll be £13.95. Our delivery man will have change up to £20.
Customer	_____
Pizza man	It should be with you in half an hour. Thank you. Bye-bye.
Customer	_____

Vocabulary

1 **Choose the word that does not belong in each group and say why.**

1	bitter	tasty	greasy	sickly
2	rich	large	extra-large	enormous
3	balanced	fast food	healthy	low-fat
4	nuts	vegetarian	fries	chocolate bars

2 2/29 **Listen to the definitions and choose the correct word.**

allergy	bill	have a sweet tooth	hot	portion	take-out

1 _____

2 _____

3 _____

4 _____

5 _____

6 _____

Pronunciation

3 **Find the group of consonants in each word and practise saying them.**

ketchup   mustard   cheeseburger   sausages

4a **Find these words in the Phrase bank. How do you pronounce them?**

/ˈreɡjʊlə(r)/   /ˈɒrɪndʒ dʒuːs/   /ˌvedʒəˈteəriən/

/ˈsɒsɪdʒɪz/   /prəˈdjuːst/   /ˈɡriːsi/

4b 2/30 **Listen and check.**

Functional language

5a **Put the words of this dialogue in the correct order.**

Customer chicken / Hi, / to / I'd / a / salad / like / eat / sandwich / in.
_____

Assistant Sure, / brown / you / want / or / white / do / bread / ?
_____

Customer please / . / Brown, _____

Assistant else / Anything / that / ? / with _____

Customer Could / cappuccino, / have / a / I / please / ? _____

Assistant Is / or / a / regular / cappuccino / ? / large / that _____

Customer please / . / Regular, _____

Assistant please / . / £4.59 / OK, / that's _____

Customer are / . / Here / you / Thanks / . _____

5b 2/31 **Listen and check.**

6 💬 **Practise the dialogue in 5a in pairs.**

 Now watch the DVD episode Eating out

12

Young workers

Phrase bank

responsibility
authority
team member
owner
leader
spending money
save up for

part-time job
night shifts
Saturday job
holiday job
cash-in-hand
National Insurance
   contributions
tax

Culture

In the USA and Britain, it's common for teenagers and university students to have a part-time job. Most work for spending money, or because they want to save up for a big purchase like a computer or a motorbike.

Vocabulary: jobs

1 Read word pairs 1-3. What is the difference between them?

1 boss / colleague

2 employer / employee

3 full-time work / part-time work

2 ⬭ In pairs, discuss questions 1-4

1 Do you have a job?

2 Do you know any people of your age who work?

3 What type of jobs do they do?

4 What's the minimum age you have to be to work in your country?

3 Read definitions 1-9. Match them to words and expressions in the Phrase bank.

1 a job you do one day a week, at the weekend _____

2 payment in notes and coins without any deductions _____

3 deductions from their income for pensions and state benefits, etc _____

4 a job you do for a few hours each day _____

5 money deducted by the government to pay for services such as education and roads _____

6 a job in which the working hours are anti-social _____

7 a job done during school or university vacations _____

8 money to use whenever you want _____

9 accumulate money in order to buy something _____

4 2/32 Listen to information about young people working in Britain. Are the statements true or false?

1 Young people can start work at the age of 14. ___

2 There are different rules for younger teenagers. ___

3 Young people cannot work in shops. ___

4 Teenage workers are not obliged to pay taxes. ___

Speaking: pay and conditions

1 **Read the jobs in the Phrase bank. Which ones are common jobs for young people in your country?**

2 **Listen to four young workers. Find their photos and write the jobs they do.**

Name: *Shahid*   Name: *Lucy*   Name: *Henry*   Name: *Natalie*

Job: _____ Job: _____ Job: _____ Job: _____

3 **Listen again. What do the workers like and dislike about their jobs?**

4 💬 **Work in pairs to discuss one of the jobs from the box below. Decide who is Student A and Student B, then read your roles. Change roles and repeat.**

---

assistant in a shoe shop   babysitter   kitchen worker in a café
assistant in a hairdresser's   football coach for a children's team   pizza deliverer

---

Student A

You are working in one of the jobs in the box.

Student B

Read the questions below. Add one more. Interview your partner.

- What's your name?
- How old are you?
- What's your job?
- Tell me about the hours you work.
- What do you like about your job?
- What do you dislike about it?

Phrase bank

shop assistant
ski instructor
newspaper boy/girl
shelf stacker
barman/barwoman
fast food attendant
pizza delivery person
clerical assistant
waiter

Language note

holiday job   vacation work

To talk about our work, we say:

I'm a shop assistant.

~~I'm shop assistant.~~

Pronunciation

Easily confused sounds

a **Which of the words in bold has the /ɔː/ sound and which has the /ɜː/ sound?**

I **wa**lk round and deliver newspapers.

I sometimes **wor**k there at weekends.

b **Listen to and say the words. Write them under the correct heading.**

birthday	four	her
learn	more	skirt
talk	water	word

work /ɜː/	*walk* /ɔː/
_____	_____

Phrase bank

au pair
lifeguard
petrol pump attendant
camp counsellor
earn money
get work experience
learn to be responsible
work in a team

Listening: summer jobs

1. _____

2. _____
3. _____
4. _____

1 Look at the photos of teenagers in the USA doing different summer jobs. Label the photos with job titles from the Phrase bank.

2 Read the words in the box. How do you say them in your language?

| requirements | employment | be on call | 24/7 |

3 (2/35) Listen to an interview about two typical summer jobs in the USA. Complete an information card about each job.

Job 1

Job title:

Requirements for post:

Job 2

Job title:

Requirements for post:

Language note

CV or
curriculum
vitae

résumé

4 (2/35) Listen again and decide if the statements are true or false.

1 To do Job 1, you are more likely to work alone if the job is in a hotel. ___

2 To do Job 1, you have to pass some rigorous physical tests if you want to work in a water park. ___

3 Job 2 allows you to choose the hours you want to work. ___

4 One of the advantages of Job 2, apart from working with other people of your age, is that your food and accommodation are provided free. ___

5 💬 Which of the jobs mentioned in the interview would you prefer? Work in pairs to discuss your choices.

Functional language: job enquiries

Students working as theme park attendants in their holidays.

Language note

We use formal language to enquire about jobs in an interview situation.

~~How much do you pay?~~

Could you tell me about the pay and conditions?

Phrase bank

Could you tell me about the pay and conditions?

What kind of qualities and skills would the ideal candidate have?

What does the job involve?

Can you tell me something about the hours of work?

Pronunciation

Word stress

a (2/36) Read the words and mark the stress on them. Listen and check.

requirements   résumé
attendant   curriculum
assistant   admission
repetitive

b Try to repeat the pronunciation using the same stress.

1 Read the Language note and Phrase bank to complete the table below.

Informal questions	Interview questions
What do you have to do?	•
What type of person do you need to be?	•
Do you have to work long hours?	•
What's the money like?	•

2 Read phrases 1–6. Decide if they represent opinions about a job (O), job requirements (R) or how you do a job (H). Label each phrase appropriately.

1 'you have to be a good swimmer' _____

2 'you work independently' _____

3 'the money's not great' _____

6 'you have to pass a lot of physical tests' _____

5 'you'll work as part of a team' _____

4 'it's quite hard work' _____

3 💬 Work in pairs to discuss a summer job. Decide who is Student A and Student B, then read your roles.

Student A
You are a manager at a theme park.

Student B
You are interested in a job at a theme park. Read the information on the card. Ask Student A about the job. Remember to use appropriate language.

Job title: *Theme park attendant*

Requirements: *have previous experience working with children, be responsible*

Good things about the job: *meet people from other countries, free admission to the park, free tickets for family and friends*

Bad things: *pay, long hours, repetitive work*

Final task: exchanging information about jobs

1 **Work in pairs. Prepare to ask someone informally about a job.**
Write 8-10 questions. Use the notes below to help you.

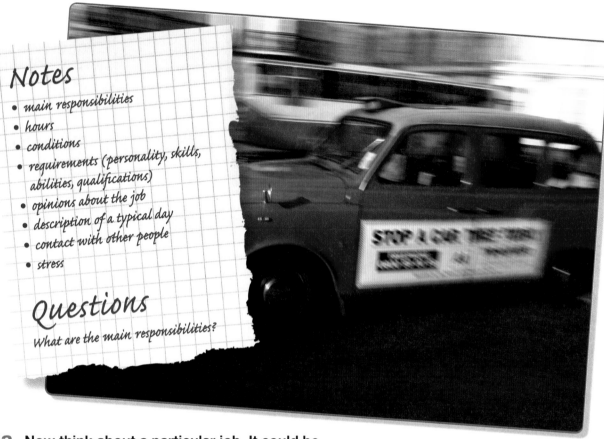

Notes
- main responsibilities
- hours
- conditions
- requirements (personality, skills, abilities, qualifications)
- opinions about the job
- description of a typical day
- contact with other people
- stress

Questions
What are the main responsibilities?

2a **Now think about a particular job. It could be …**

1 your dream job.

2 a friend or relative's job (for example your mother's job).

3 one of the job profiles from pages 72-73.

2b **Think about what this job involves. Use your questions from 1 to help you.**

3 **Work in pairs. Ask each other about your jobs.**

4 **Now work in pairs again to discuss the pros and cons of different professions.**
Decide who is Student A and Student B, then read your roles.

Student A

You are going to ask Student B about their job.
Use the questions you wrote in 1 to help you.

Student B

Turn to page 105. Choose either job A or job B to talk about.

Read the Strategy box and try to give balanced answers to Student A's questions.

Strategy

2/37 Listen to the extract from page 72.

'The money's not great, but your food and accommodation are free.'

Notice how the speaker attempts to balance a negative comment with a positive point. Try to do this when people ask you about school or work.

Vocabulary

1 (2/38) **Listen and classify the words you hear. Write them in the correct groups.**

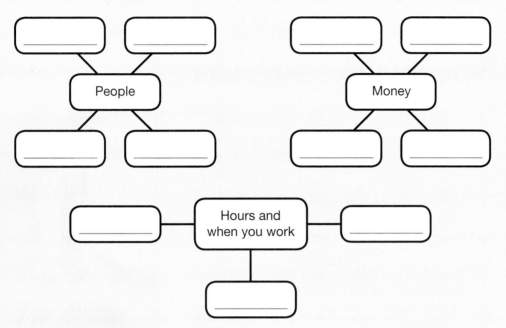

People

Money

Hours and when you work

Pronunciation

2 (2/39) **Listen and circle the word you hear.**

1 walk   work
2 bought   Bert
3 saw   sir
4 born   burn
5 bored   bird
6 four   fur

3 💬 **Work in pairs. Student A says one of the two words in 1. Student B points to the word.**

Functional language

4 **Dean has a summer job taking family groups on tours at an aquarium. Complete the interview about his job.**

Question	kind / qualities and skills / need?
Dean	need / know about marine life; have / pass tests.
Question	What / job / involve?
Dean	Work / public; work / team.
Question	Work / hours?
Dean	OK / 10-6.
Question	Money?
Dean	Quite good; great experience.

5 💬 **Work in pairs to practise the dialogue.**

Phrase bank

responsibility
authority
team member
owner
leader
spending money
save up for
part-time job
night shifts
Saturday job
holiday job
cash in hand
National Insurance
  contributions
tax

shop assistant
ski instructor
newspaper boy/girl
shelf stacker
barman/barwoman
fast food attendant
pizza delivery person
clerical assistant
waiter

lifeguard
camp counsellor
petrol pump attendant
theme park attendant
au pair
earn money
get work experience
learn to be responsible
work in a team

Could you tell me
  about the pay and
  conditions?
What kind of qualities
  and skills are you
  looking for?
What does the job
  involve?
Can you tell me
  something about the
  hours of work?

 Now watch the DVD episode Getting a job   **75**

13

University of life

Phrase bank

hitchhiking
inter-railing
backpacking

journey   travel
travelling   trip

break   defer
employment   gap year
life experience
school-leavers
take a year out
volunteering

2. ____

Language note

I went on a great trip to the USA last year.

~~I went on a great travel to the USA last year.~~

Trip is a noun used to talk about a holiday or excursion where you go and come back.

Travel is normally used as a verb though it can also be a noun.

Journey is a noun we use to emphasize the act of travelling, especially to talk about the duration or method of transport.

Vocabulary: experiences

1 **Label the photos on this page with the words below then answer the questions.**

hitchhiking   inter-railing   backpacking

1   What are the pros and cons of these different ways of travelling?
2   Have you tried any of them? Would you like to?

2 **Read the Language note then complete sentences 1-4 with words from the Phrase bank.**

1   How long does your _____ to school take?
2   Within Spain, do you prefer to _____ by plane, car or train?
3   Would you like to go on a _____ round Europe?
4   If you could spend a few months _____ where would you go?

3 🔊 2/40 **Read the text and complete it with the words in the box. Listen and check.**

> defer   gap year   employment   life experience   a break
> take a year out   travelling   volunteering   school-leavers

Taking a (1) _____ is now an increasingly popular activity for many young people in Britain, according to a recent report. Every year, around a quarter of school leavers who are going on to university decide to (2) _____ the start of their course and (3) _____ before starting their degree course. Some do it to get work or (4) _____, others just want to take (5) _____ from their studies.

Some teenagers spend the year (6) _____ in schools, hospitals or NGOs in the UK or abroad. Others prefer to spend part of the year working to save up money and then spend several months (7) _____. South America, Asia and Australia are popular destinations.

Gap years aren't only for (8) _____ – some people take a career break later in life, but they are certainly most popular with 16–25 year olds. Annually around 250,000 British people in this age-group take a gap year. It's very popular in countries like Britain and Australia and becoming more typical in the US, but in other countries like Japan there's more pressure on young people to go straight from education into (9) _____.

3. ____

Speaking: really useful experiences

1 **Find two expressions in the Phrase bank that match the definitions.**

1 a unique or very rare event

2 dramatically informative

1. _____

2. _____

3. _____

4. _____

Phrase bank

a real eye-opener
a once-in-a-lifetime
   experience
...your attitude
...something count
...a difference
...your view of the
   world
...a contribution
...your perspective on
   life

volunteering
third world
work experience

Language note

Change your way of thinking

~~Change your chip~~

2 **Look at the photos. Match what the people are saying to each photo.**

1 'I'm on a working holiday in Australia.'

2 'I'm back-packing round Asia.'

3 'I wanted to get some work experience before my degree.'

4 'I wanted to spend some time doing voluntary work.'

3 2/41 **Listen to the people talking about their gap year experiences. Write the speaker's name on their photo.**

4 **Write words from the Phrase bank that collocate with the verbs.**

change _____   make _a difference_
_____   _____

5 🗩 **Work in pairs to discuss what you would like to do on a gap year. Use the ideas below and expressions from 4.**

- how you would spend your time
- where you would go
- how you would finance your year
- what you think you would learn from the experience.

Pronunciation

/ə/ sound

a 2/42 Read the sentence from exercise 3. Listen to how the underlined words are pronounced.

I decided to take a year out and come to Australia before I start studying to be a vet next autumn.

b Read the sentence below and underline the words you think have the /ə/ sound.

I'm going to do business studies next year so I was really pleased to get a job in an advertising agency.

c 2/43 Listen and check. Practise reading the sentence paying attention to the /ə/ sound.

study abroad
exchange programme
European Union
cultural exchange
student residence
university course
teaching styles
hands-on approach

Listening: Erasmus

ERASMUS FOR EVERYONE

Every year the Erasmus programme enables students in 31 European countries to study abroad. There are lots of reasons for taking a year as an Erasmus student – here are our top five:

1 It's a great addition to your CV and will help you stand out in the job market.

2 You can improve your language skills.

3 You'll meet people from around the world.

4 It's a chance to discover a new culture and get a more international perspective.

5 You'll learn a lot more than just the subject you study at university.

Raquel Cánovas is from Madrid. Last year she studied at the Galway-Mayo Institute of Technology (GMIT) in Galway, Ireland.

Culture

Galway is an historic city in County Galway, Ireland. It is located on Ireland's west coast. It is often described as the most Irish of the island's cities, as both English and the native Gaelic are spoken there.

Galway

Dublin

1 **Read the website about the Erasmus programme and answer the questions.**

1 What kind of student is the Erasmus programme for?

2 Which of the suggested reasons for joining the Erasmus programme do you think are most important?

2 2/44 **Listen to Raquel talk about her experiences. Choose the correct answer.**

1 Raquel says that while she was in GMIT she …

   a mainly spoke Spanish with other Erasmus students.

   b spoke English most of the time.

   c spoke Gaelic with local people.

2 While she was at GMIT, Raquel …

   a shared a bedroom with another student.

   b lived in student accommodation.

   c shared a house with students from different countries.

3 The classes were different from what Raquel was used to because …

   a they were easier than her classes in Madrid.

   b the class sizes were bigger.

   c they involved a lot of listening and taking notes.

4 Two other differences that Raquel mentions are …

   a the people and the prices.

   b the weather and the length of the day.

   c the length of the day and the prices.

Functional language: eliciting

1 (2/45) Use the Phrase bank to complete the interviewer's questions. Then listen and check.

1 Can you tell us ...
2 Why's that ...
3 First of all English, ...
4 Tell me about ...
5 That must ...
6 And I imagine it was interesting ...
7 What were the main differences ...
8 Can you give us ...
9 Do you have any ...

Interviews with Erasmus students

2 Answer the questions about what the interviewer said.

1 Which phrases are questions?
2 Which phrase is an imperative?
3 Which are statements that act as questions?

3 Read the interview about a trip to Morocco. Can you guess what the interviewer asked?

Interviewer Can you tell me something about your trip to Marrakesh?

Student Well, it was amazing – everything was so different!

Interviewer _____?

Student Well, the people, the way of life ... even the shopping!

Interviewer Oh yes, _____.

Student Well, the markets are incredible. They're huge, it's really easy to get lost. You can buy all kinds of clothes, bags ...

Interviewer Wow! _____?

Student Yes, but you have to haggle, you know, argue about the price.

Interviewer I don't think I'd be good at that. _____?

Student Well, it is quite stressful: it's all very fast-moving and in your face, so it's not the most relaxing type of holiday. But it was a brilliant experience.

4 (2/46) Listen and check.

5 Practise reading the dialogue in 3, paying attention to the intonation.

6 Work in pairs to discuss a place you have visited. Try to elicit more detail from each other.

Phrase bank

...I imagine.
...any examples?
...the people you met
...exactly?
...you noticed between life in Galway and Madrid?
...attending a foreign university?
...regrets?
...something about that?
...have been interesting?

Culture

The currency in Ireland is the Euro. When talking about prices they use the singular.

'It costs ten euro'

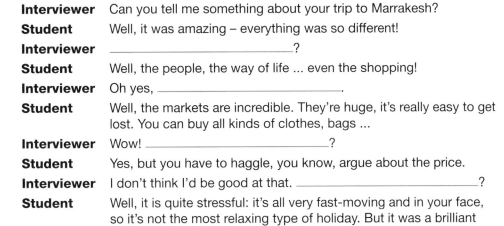

Language note

attend lectures
~~assist to university classes~~

Pronunciation

Intonation

a (2/47) Listen to what the interviewer said then answer the questions below.

That must have been interesting.

b 1. Does the first speaker's intonation rise or fall?

2. Does the second speaker's intonation rise or fall?

Final task: highlighting your experience

1 **Listen to two people in job interviews talking about the value of their gap years. Which speaker is better at highlighting the positive aspects of their experience?**

Strategy

When you want to persuade someone of the value of your experience, give specific examples of activities or events to support your point.

2 Read the arguments for taking a year out.

1 "You can make a difference by doing voluntary work."

2 "It changes your view of the world."

3 "You get some work experience."

4 "Improve your CV and job prospects."

5 "Meet different kinds of people."

6 "Practise languages and learn new ones."

7 "Travel and experience other cultures."

8 "Take a break from academic study."

3 Choose the six arguments in 2 that you think are the most important. Write a reason to justify each choice.

4 Work in pairs to compare your choices and discuss your reasons. Together, choose the four arguments you think are most important.

5 Work in pairs. Imagine you are in a job interview. Decide who is Student A and Student B, then read your roles. Change roles and repeat.

Student A

You are the employer. Ask the candidate about their gap year.

Use eliciting techniques to explore their experience.

Student B

You are the job candidate. Choose one of the options below and think how you can 'sell' the value of your experience to your potential employer. Remember you can include arguments from 2.

Option 1 - You spent three months in the USA as a classroom assistant, helping to teach Spanish in a primary school.

Option 2 - You spent three months as a ski instructor in the Pyrenees and three months teaching surfing in Tarifa.

Option 3 - You worked on reception in your uncle's hotel for six months, then went to the beach for a month with your friends.

Vocabulary

1 Match the words to make expressions.

1	a once in a	a	year
2	a real	b	year out
3	defer	c	your degree
4	gap	d	eye-opener
5	take a	e	lifetime experience

2 Use your answers to 1 to complete sentences 1-5.

1 When I was 18, I spent a year on a sheep farm in Australia. It was a ____.

2 Working in a hospital as a volunteer last summer was a _____. I didn't realize how stressful it is.

3 Are you are a sixth former? Fed up with studying? Don't give up your dreams of a university course permanently. _____ for a year.

4 "I took a _____ between school and university. I'll never regret it, I learned so much."

5 It's not just students who _____ when they need a change. Adults do too.

3 Correct the mistake in each sentence.

1 My brother spent last year doing auto-stop round Europe.

2 Travelling is a very good way for young people to put off new experiences.

3 I don't like packbacking – it's very tiring.

4 My cousin worked as a volunteering in India.

Pronunciation

4 2/49 Underline the schwa sounds /ə/ in the sentences, then practise saying them. Listen and check.

1 I had a Saturday job all the way through sixth form, and I worked in a factory for three months to save up for the trip.

2 Going to study at a university in another city and finding somewhere to stay there is a real challenge.

3 I think it's brilliant to have the chance to live in a different country.

4 It's incredible, you go into a market and you realize it's huge. It's really easy to get lost.

Functional language

5 Compare and contrast one of the pairs.

1 going on holiday with your parents / going on holiday with friends

2 inter-railing / travelling by plane

3 spending a holiday at the coast / spending a holiday in your family village

Phrase bank

hitchhiking
inter-railing
backpacking

journey   travel
travelling   trip

break   defer
employment
gap year
life experience
school-leavers
take a year out
volunteering

A difference
A contribution
make something count
your attitude
your view of the world
your perspective on life
a once-in-a-lifetime
   experience
a real eye-opener
volunteering
third world
work experience

study abroad
exchange programme
European Union
cultural exchange
student residence
university course
teaching styles
hands-on approach

And it must be cheaper
   than here
And the food, I
   suppose.
For example?
Tell me about the
   markets.
Was there anything you
   didn't like?

🔘 **Now watch the DVD episode Gap years**

14

Travel

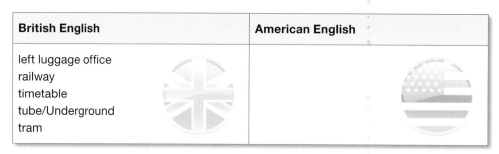

1. _____
2. _____
3. _____

Phrase bank

bus
coach
plane
train
ferry

subway
schedule
railroad
baggage check
street car

fare
first class
outward journey
period return
student travel-card

Vocabulary:
travel options

1 Use the Phrase bank to label the travel options in the photos. What do you like and dislike about each way of travelling?

2 There are important differences between British and American English. Use the Phrase bank to complete the table.

British English	American English
left luggage office	
railway	
timetable	
tube/Underground	
tram	

Language note

single   one way
return   round trip

The person who checks your ticket on a train is called a guard.

The person who checks your ticket on a bus is called a conductor.

3 Read the definitions. Find words and expressions from the Phrase bank to match each definition.

1 a ticket that allows you to come back some time after initially travelling _____

2 the price you pay to travel _____

3 the first part of a round trip _____

4 a document that gives a discount to a traveller in full-time education _____

5 a more expensive way to travel that offers better seats and service _____

4 2/50 Use the words in 3 to complete the text from a guidebook. Listen and check.

HOME	ENGLAND	SCOTLAND	WALES	N. IRELAND	FORUM

The first thing you need to know about travel in the UK is that there are several railway companies offering different prices and options. It's important to ask for the best deal before you buy your ticket. Normally the ticket clerk will give you a standard ticket so please tell them if you want to travel (1) _____.

The time you travel is also a factor. For example, if you're coming back to the departure station on the same day as your (2) _____, you should ask for a day return, but if you're going to come back days or weeks later, you need a (3) _____.

Students should bear in mind that they will often pay a cheaper (4) _____ if they can demonstrate that they are in full time education through showing a (5) _____.

Speaking: getting to London

Phrase bank

passport control
baggage reclaim area
arrivals hall
rail-travellers'
    information centre

non-stop service
stopping service
mainline station
journey time
railcard
ticket machines
transport system
overground
scheduled stops
direction of travel
destination

1 (2/51) **Number the photos in the order in which you hear the people speak.**

2 **Read word pairs 1-3. What is the difference between them?**

1 a tube station/a main-line station
2 a direct service/a stopping service
3 an eastbound train/a southbound train

3 (2/52) **Listen to a tourist talking to a tourist information officer. Which form of transport does he take and why?**

4 (2/52) **Listen to the dialogue again and complete the table.**

	Heathrow Express	Heathrow Connect	London Underground
How often do the trains go?			
How long does it take?			
How much does it cost?			

Culture

In most cities in the UK, local people use a travel card for bus or tube travel. In London this is called an Oyster card.

5a 💬 **Work in pairs. Decide who is Student A and Student B, then read your roles.**

Student A

You are at Heathrow Airport, London. You want to travel into London. Ask for information.

Student B

You are the clerk at the ticket office.

Answer the questions Student A asks. Use the answers in 4.

5b **Repeat the task with new roles.**

Student A

You are an information officer at your nearest airport.

Student B

You are an English visitor to Madrid.

Pronunciation 🔊

Stress on numbers

a (2/53) **Listen to the numbers and complete the pronunciation rules.**

The stress on the numbers 13, 14, 15 is on the **first/second** syllable.

The stress on the numbers 30, 40, 50 is on the **first/second** syllable.

b (2/54) **Listen and circle the number you hear.**

13 30   17 70   18 80
14 40   16 60

Phrase bank

aisle seat
window seat
advance booking
telephone booking
internet rate
validate your ticket

Culture

York is an important, historic city in the north of England. Its many associations with battles and invasions have helped the city to win the title of 'the most haunted city in Europe'.

York

Language note

arrive in York

get to York

~~arrive to York~~

Listening: northbound

CITY OF YORK

Gillygate
Monkgate
Lord Mayors Walk
Petergate
York Minster
National Railway Museum
Station Road
Market Street
The Shambles
Jorvic Viking Centre
Bridge Street
Castlegate
Walmgate
York Railway Station
River Ouse
City wall
Bishopgate Street

Situated in north-east England, the city of **York** has historical connections with Roman, Viking and Medieval culture.
Here are just some of the things you can do here:
• visit the magnificent cathedral of York Minster
• find out about Viking life at the Jorvik Viking Centre
• visit the National Railway Museum
• go shopping in The Shambles

1 2/55 **Listen to Ravi's voicemail message to Maria about what they are going to do in York. Which of the places on the map does Ravi not mention?**

2 2/56 **Listen to Maria booking her trip to York. Answer the questions.**

1 Maria's bus leaves at …
  a half past ten.
  b nine o'clock.
  c half past nine.

2 Her journey will take …
  a under 5 hours.
  b between 5 and 6 hours.
  c over 6 hours.

3 She decides to buy…
  a a single ticket.
  b a return ticket.
  c an open ticket.

4 Maria thinks the young person's travel card …
  a is an example of how expensive things are in the UK.
  b would save her money on her trip to York.
  c would only be of interest to her if she lived in the UK.

5 The bus leaves from bay …
  a 3.
  b 13.
  c 30.

3 2/57 **Listen to Maria's call to Ravi. Are the statements true or false? Correct any false statements.**

1 Ravi tells Maria that he will meet her when her bus gets to York.
2 Maria will text Ravi if she decides not to go.

Functional language: reservations

1 Read the sentences from when Maria booked her bus journey.

I'd like to **book** a seat to York.

Er, well, no, **I don't think so**.

Do you want **a single or a return**?

I'll take an open ticket.

The journey time is 5 hours and 15 minutes.

What time does that **get into** York?

Where does it **leave** from?

Would you like a window or an aisle seat?

2 Write a phrase in bold from 1 that means the same as the expressions below.

1	arrive in	5	reserve
2	one-way or round-trip	6	no, thanks
3	I'd like	7	it takes
4	do you want to sit by	8	depart

3 Read the words in the Phrase bank and find ...

1 three words to describe types of ticket _____ _____ _____

2 three places to get on or off public transport _____ _____ _____

3 three types of seat on public transport _____ _____ _____

4 two phrases for describing times of travel _____ _____

4 💬 Work in pairs. Decide who is Student A and Student B, then read your roles.

Student A

You are an English person travelling in Germany.

You want to find out how to travel from Berlin to Munich.

Prepare some questions to ask Student B.

Student B

You are a tourist information officer in Berlin who can speak English.

Respond to Student A's questions.

Phrase bank

aisle seat
window seat
forward-facing seat
platform
bay
stop
book
reserve
single
return
open ticket
off-peak
rush hour

Culture

In the UK, ticket prices on buses, coaches and trains are cheaper for young people and students. In London, buses are free for people in full-time education or anyone under the age of 16.

Pronunciation

/aɪ/ and /eɪ/ sounds

a Read the words. Do they contain the /aɪ/ sound or the /eɪ/ sound?

bay arrivals rail aisle main I'll train line

b 2/58 Listen to the words in a, then write them under the correct headings.

/aɪ/   /eɪ/

Final task: booking a trip

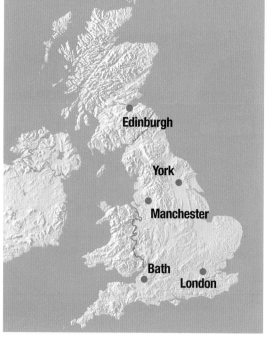

1a (2/59) **Listen to the travel information questions. How does the intonation on the words in bold change?**

1 Is that **morning** or **evening**?

2 Do you want a **single** or a **return**?

3 Would you like a **window** or an **aisle seat**?

1b 💬 Practise reading the questions with the same intonation.

2 💬 Work in pairs. Decide who is Student A and Student B. Read Task 1 and do the activity.

3 Change roles. Read Task 2 and do the activity.

Task 1

Student A

You want to get from London to Bath tomorrow morning and return the following Tuesday afternoon.

You want to know the different travel options for train and coach before buying your ticket.

Prepare questions about times and prices.

Read the strategy box.

Student B

You work at a visitors' information centre.

Read the transport information on page 106 before you start.

Remember to use the correct intonation in any questions you ask.

Task 2

Student B

You want to get from Manchester to York tomorrow morning and return the following Wednesday afternoon.

You want to know the different travel options for train and coach before buying your ticket.

Prepare questions about times and prices.

Read the strategy box.

Student A

You work at a visitor information centre. Look at the transport information on page 106 before you start

Remember to use the correct intonation in any questions you ask.

Strategy

When preparing to ask questions about travel, write these headings and leave space to note the answers.

Destination

Train times

Coach times

Leaves from

Prices

After you have noted down the information, repeat it back aloud so that the person you are speaking to can correct any errors.

Vocabulary

1 **Read the words and classify them. Write them in the correct groups.**

| aisle | bay | fare | first class | internet rate | left luggage office |
| mainline station | one-way | open return | platform | student railcard |

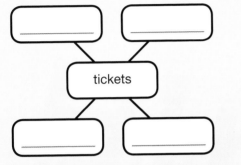

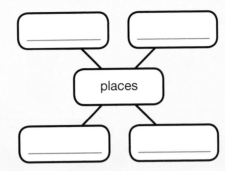

2 **Correct these sentences by changing the word in bold.**

1 In the USA a return ticket is called a **two-way** ticket.

2 A southbound train is travelling from the **south**.

3 A tube station is the same as a **mainline** station.

4 A **direct train** stops at stations on the way.

Pronunciation

3 💬 **Work in pairs. Choose six of the numbers. Say them to your partner.**

13   60   70   18   80   30   14   16   90   50   15   40   17   19

4a **Find these words in the Phrase bank. How do you pronounce them?**

/treɪn/   /pleɪn/   /reɪt/   /ˈvælɪdeɪt/   /aɪl/   /beɪ/   /baɪ/

4b (2/60) **Listen and check.**

Functional language

5 **Put the sentences of the dialogue in a logical order.**

I'd like a ticket to Oxford, please. _1_

A single, please. ___

Go up over the bridge. ___

Here you are. What time's the next train? ___

How do I get there? ___

Is that a single or a return? ___

OK – which platform's that? ___

OK, great. Thanks. ___

Platform 2, it's on the other side. ___

That's £4.29 please. ___

There's one at half past. ___

6 💬 **Practise reading the dialogue in 5 with a partner. Close your books. Try to say it from memory.**

Phrase bank

bus   coach
plane   train
ferry   subway
schedule
railroad
baggage check
street car
fare
first class
outward journey
period return
student railcard

passport control
baggage reclaim area
arrivals hall
rail-travellers'
   information centre
non-stop service
stopping service
mainline station
journey time
railcard
ticket machines
transport system
overground
scheduled stops
direction of travel
destination
The world is your
   oyster

aisle seat
window seat
advance booking
telephone booking
internet rate
Validate your ticket

forward-facing seat
platform
bay   stop
book   reserve
single   return
open ticket
off-peak
rush hour

Prepare to ...
describe a photo

Oral exam. Describing photos.

Task: Look at the photos. Talk about the similarities and differences between them. Speculate about how you think the people feel and say which situation you would prefer.

1 Look at the photos and read the task. How would you answer it?

2 (2/61) Listen to a student answering the task in 1. In pairs, discuss how well the student responded to the task.

3a (2/62) Listen to another student answering the task. What does she say when she doesn't remember the word for something?

3b (2/62) Listen to the second speaker again and decide if the statements are true or false. Give reasons to support your answers.

1   The speaker says that the first difference is about when the events are taking place. ___
2   The speaker thinks the first photo could be of some type of industrial action. ___
3   The speaker thinks this is an effective way of getting what you want. ___
4   The speaker thinks the people might feel satisfied in the second situation. ___
5   The speaker sees a similarity in the objective of the two groups of people. ___
6   The speaker would choose to be in the second situation. ___

Remember: Unit 10

In Unit 10 you prepared to compare and contrast photos. Write as many phrases as you can for each category below.

Describing similarities   *Both the pictures are ...*
Describing differences   *In the first picture we can see X, whereas ...*

4 Read the words for talking about events. Write them under the appropriate headings.

a get-together   a great atmosphere   a wedding anniversary   backing singers
an amazing performance   candidates   different generations   fans
get back in touch   a grandstand   a home crowd   an invigilator   a support band
a stadium   keep an eye on the time   nervous tension   play an encore

a sporting event	a family celebration	a public examination	a concert

5 Think of a time when you attended one of the events in the table. Prepare notes to help you describe your experience.

6 💬 Work in pairs. Decide who is Student A and Student B, then read your roles.

Checklist ✔

Comparing photos

Remember to …

1 Give more than one similarity and difference between the photos.

2 Speculate about what might be happening in the photo, where people might be and how they might feel.

3 Give your opinion about the photo, explaining the reasons for your opinion.

Task

Student A

You are going to describe the photos on this page.

Talk about the similarities and differences between them. Say how you think the people feel in each one, and which situation you'd prefer to be in and why.

Student B

You are going to describe the photos on page 106.

Talk about the similarities and differences between them. Say how you think the people feel in each one, and which situation you'd prefer to be in and why.

Prepare to...
have a formal debate

1 🔲 **Look at the pictures. Work in pairs to discuss what you can see.**

2 (2/63) **Listen to the first part of a description of a formal debate and decide if the statements are true or false. Give reasons to support your answers.**

1 A formal debate is just like an uncontrolled argument.

2 Lots of people consider debating to be a hobby.

3 The motion is always something in the news at the present time.

4 In a debate there are generally two teams called Affirmative and Negative.

5 The main parts of the debate are presenting your arguments and arguing against the other team's points.

6 Your team will get extra marks if you personally criticize the speakers of the opposing team.

3 (2/64) **Now listen to the second part of the description and complete statements 1-3 using words from the box.**

> rebut (x2)   state   restate   sum up the team's argument

1 The first speakers on each team take turns to _____ their team's argument.

2 The second speakers on each team take turns to _____ their teams argument, and _____ the opposing team's argument.

3 The third speakers take turns to _____ but they don't _____ the other team's argument.

4 (2/65) **Listen to details of the judging process and complete the descriptions of a formal debate.**

1 _____ marks are given for the content of the argument. This is called the 'matter'.

2 The way in which the speakers develop and organize their argument is called the _____. There are _____ marks available for this.

3 The conduct of the speakers is called their 'manner' and there are _____ marks available for this.

Task

The motion is ...

It is time to end the dominance of football on TV. Discuss.

5 Read the task box. Think about how you feel about the motion.

6 Once your teacher has divided you into teams, prepare your arguments. Use the checklist to help you.

Checklist ☑

Planning

Use the internet to research facts for your argument.

Organization

Decide who is going to speak and when.

Sequence the main points of your argument.

Practice

Rehearse each person's speech

Try to predict what the other team will argue and practise your responses.

Remember: Units 5 and 10

a In Unit 5 and Unit 10, you practised using linking expressions. Write the formal equivalents of the following ...

• to start off with   • another reason is   • I also think

b Check your answers on pages 28-33 and 58-63.

Prepare to...
do a project

1 📢 Look at photos A–C of some traditional events in Britain. Work in pairs to compare and contrast the photos.

A. Royal Ascot horse races.

B. Summer solstice celebrations, Stonehenge.

C. The Highland Games, Scotland.

2 2/66 Listen to three people talking about the events in the photos and answer the questions.

	Which event do they describe?	What were the other people like?	Did the speaker enjoy it?
Speaker 1			
Speaker 2			
Speaker 3			

3 2/66 Listen again. Write A, B or C to indicate which photo sentences 1-7 refer to.

1 Clothes played an important part. ___ ___
2 There's a spiritual side to the event. ___
3 It has connections with the past. ___ ___
4 The event happens at a particular time of day. ___
5 There was a sporting element to the event. ___ ___
6 Social status was important. ___
7 There was a musical element to the event. ___

4 📢 In pairs, answer the questions.

1 Which event would you most like to attend and why?
2 What traditional events have you been to in your country?
3 What did you like or dislike about them?
4 Do you think it is important to maintain traditions? Why/why not?

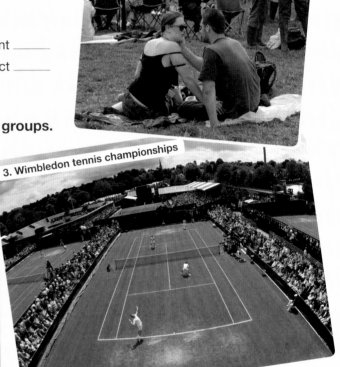

1. Glastonbury music festival

5 Read the words to describe what is happening in
photos 1-3. Write 1, 2 or 3 to indicate which photo
you associate with each word or phrase.

amateur theatre groups _____ buskers _____

camping _____ cosy venues _____ trophy _____

international championship _____ knockout tournament _____

main stage _____ street performers _____ support act _____

to headline _____ top level players _____

6 Read the project box. Work in pairs or small groups.
Plan a visit to one of the events.

2. Edinburgh fringe festival

3. Wimbledon tennis championships

Remember: Units 5 and 10

a **In Unit 5, you prepared to discuss plans for a weekend. Write any expressions you
can remember for...**

• making suggestions   • agreeing and disagreeing

b **In Unit 10, you prepared to present a campaign. Write any expressions you can
remember for...**

• explaining the reasons for your ideas   • describing the different aspects of your plan

Reference section

Contents

DVD Quiz: Leaving school

Did you know?

Around 80% of university students in the UK live away from home.
This is considered an important part of the university experience.

Watch the episode then complete the quiz.

Section 1

1 How long are most UK degree courses?
2 How much time do students on a degree course such as nursing spend doing work experience?

Section 2

3 What is the name of Ed's friend?
4 What does Ed's friend want to study?
5 What A levels is Ed doing?
6 What industry does Ed want to work in?

Section 3

7 In which city is Emma studying?
8 How long has Emma been at university?
9 Complete the phrase Emma uses to say that university gives you more independence: 'You're very much your …'
10 What occupation does Emma want to do when she finishes university?

DVD Quiz: Leaving home

Did you know?

In Britain, 50% of young women leave home by the age of 21, and 50% of young men leave home by the age of 23.

Watch the episode then complete the quiz.

Section 1

1 Complete the name of the accommodation where most first-year UK university students live: '… of residence'.

2 Besides shopping and cooking, which four responsibilities does the DVD mention for students who share a house or flat?

Section 2

3 Which city is Olivia studying in?

4 How does Olivia describe the process of looking for a place to live?

5 Why does the girl apologize for the kitchen?

6 How many people currently live in the house, and how many are girls?

7 Which five types of bill do the people in the house have to pay?

Section 3

8 How many boys live in Adam's flat?

9 Who owns Adam's flat?

10 In the first semester, what routine did the people in Adam's flat have on Sundays?

DVD Quiz: Appearances

Did you know?

Street markets are very popular places to buy new and second-hand clothes in the UK. London's Camden Market is one of the most popular visitor attractions, with approximately 100,000 people visiting it each weekend. Some of the most popular clothes on sale here are for teenage members of alternative sub-cultures such as goths and cybergoths.

Watch the episode then complete the quiz.

Section 1

1 According to the DVD, why do some people have a distinctive dress sense? Is it because they …

   a want to blend in?

   b are unconventional?

   c want to be comfortable?

2 What is the occasion where the people are wearing formal clothes?

Section 2

3 What job is Ed's interview for?

4 What is wrong with the first suit that Ed tries on?

5 What 'special offer' does the salesman tell Ed about?

6 How much money does Ed spend in the shop?

Section 3

7 Why is Surina wearing a hat?

8 What kind of black skirt is she wearing?

9 Surina says she likes to mix different colours and …

10 How many pairs of high-heeled shoes does Surina own?

DVD Quiz: Free time

Did you know?

Culture

Glastonbury music festival, which is held near Glastonbury in south-west England, is the world's largest open-air music festival. It covers an area of over 3.5 square kilometres, and around 170,000 people attend every year.

Watch the episode then complete the quiz.

Section 1

1 At what time of year do music festivals happen in the UK?

2 At what age can you buy alcohol in the UK?

Section 2

3 Why do Ruby and Olivia want to do something special this Saturday night?

4 Which two film types does Ruby suggest they go and see?

5 What can you do at the Basement Club?

6 What do they decide to do in the end?

7 Where did Ed see DJ Mixit play?

Section 3

8 What four things does Zoe enjoy doing in her free time?

9 How often does Zoe go to belly dancing classes?

10 What do Zoe and her friends usually do when they go out together?

DVD Quiz: Transport

Watch the episode then complete the quiz.

Section 1

1 Which young people often learn to drive as soon as they are 17?
2 Which young people are more likely to use buses?

Section 2

3 Why doesn't Ed drive to work?
4 How long does the train take to get to Marston?
5 Does he have to go on more than one train to get there?
6 Why is it a problem for him that the last train leaves at 22.45?
7 How does he solve this problem?

Section 3

8 What has William been doing for 25 years?
9 Why can't you ride a full-power motorbike in the UK when you're 18?
10 What is William's favourite motorbike …
   a a Harley Davidson?
   b a Yamaha?
   c a Triumph?

DVD Quiz: Eating out

Did you know?

The first Chinese restaurant in the UK opened in London in 1907. Today, there are many thousands of them, and nine out of ten Londoners eat more foreign food than British food!

Watch the episode then complete the quiz.

Section 1

1 What two examples of traditional British food are mentioned in the DVD?

2 Which four examples are given of exotic foreign countries or regions whose food you can eat in London?

Section 2

3 What drinks do Ed, Ruby and Olivia order?

4 Which course do they decide not to eat?

5 How does Ed want his burger to be cooked?

6 What does Olivia have for dessert?

7 How does Ruby want to pay for the bill?

Section 3

8 What time does Julia eat lunch?

9 Why do Julia and her friends like to eat in pubs?

10 Which two types of takeaway food does she usually eat?

DVD Quiz: Getting a job

Did you know?

In the UK, 13-16 year-olds may do paid work, but they mustn't work for more than 12 hours a week during term time.

Watch the episode then complete the quiz.

Section 1

1 What examples are given of things that teenagers can buy if they have a part-time job?
2 According to the DVD, what is the main advantage of work placements?

Section 2

3 What three responsibilities does the job of hotel receptionist include?
4 Which three places has Ed worked in previously?
5 What part-time job is Ed currently doing?
6 What example of Ed's work does the interviewer ask him to describe?
7 What is Ed's 'dream'?

Section 3

8 How long has Matt been a video editor?
9 What doesn't Matt like about his job?
10 What three main qualities are needed to do Matt's job?

DVD Quiz: Gap years

Did you know?

Around a quarter of UK university applicants take a gap year before going to university – though this figure has fallen slightly in recent years, probably due to worsening economic conditions.

Watch the episode then complete the quiz.

Section 1

1 Which of these activities is not part of the gap year experience …

a full-time study?

b paid work?

c travel?

d voluntary work?

2 What places are given as examples of where young people often go travelling during their gap years?

Section 2

3 What is Olivia doing tomorrow?

4 What does Ruby's mum want her to do soon?

5 What made Ed dislike education?

6 What disadvantage of taking a gap year does Olivia mention?

7 Why is Ruby's mum not very keen for Ruby to do a gap year?

Section 3

8 What countries did Kate work in during her gap year?

9 How does Kate think her gap year has changed her as a person?

10 What bad experiences did Vinay have during his gap year?

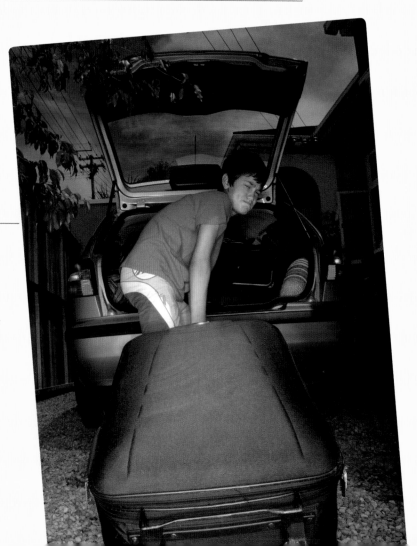

Exam tips

Watch the episode 'Exam Time'

1 Read the tips below and answer the questions.

Tip 1
Giving personal information

When giving personal information, try to make the information as complete as possible. Compare the following answers.

Student A: I'm from Cadiz … it is a city in Spain.

Student B: I'm from a small village about ten kilometres from Cadiz in the south of Spain. I've lived in Cadiz for two years but I'm originally from Sevilla.

Tip 3
Describing a photo

Remember:

1 Describe what you can see using phrases such as *In the photo there is/there are …*

2 Describe what you think is happening in the photo by saying *The children are looking at a computer.*

3 Speculate about what might be happening/ have happened/ be about to happen by saying *They might have seen something funny on the computer.*

Tip 2
Discussing the pros and cons of a proposal

Remember:

1 Use the second conditional to describe a proposal or recommendation, e.g. *A swimming pool would be great and I think lots of students would use it.*

2 Use the present simple to talk about an existing situation, e.g. *I don't think we need more computers in school because we don't have time to use them.*

3 Use the third conditional to talk about hypothetical situations, e.g. *If the government had asked students what they should have spent the money on they would have got a different answer.*

Tip 4
Concluding your description of a photograph

Remember:

Give your personal point of view or reaction, e.g. *I would prefer to be an artist rather than a doctor, but unfortunately I'm not at all creative!*

Communication activities

Audioscript, exercise 8, page 31

OK, well I'm from London and maybe I'm a bit biased, but for me, it's the best city in the world.

What makes it so great? There's so many things that it's difficult to know where to start.

To start with, I think London is a very historic city, a lot of significant things happened here and there are lots of great places to visit if you want to know more about London's past. Two places I'd really recommend are the Tower of London, where they used to imprison and then execute famous traitors, and Shakespeare's Globe theatre where there's a fascinating exhibit about life in the 16th century.

But London's also a very modern city, it's been the home to many new trends and fashions in the 20th and 21st centuries, for example there's some amazing modern architecture, as well as great clubs and venues if you want to listen to the latest sounds.

Another reason I love London is that it's a very cosmopolitan city – the people who live in London come from all over the world and some districts are strongly influenced by other cultures. You can also try food from many different countries.

I also think London is a brilliant place for tourists – there are so many fantastic museums and famous places to visit, and of course the shopping's great. Go shopping in the department stores in Oxford Street or visit the market at Camden Lock.

Are there any negative points? Well, if you don't like the busy, fast-moving rhythm of a big city, then London may not be for you, and like any big city there is quite a lot of congestion, street crime and some places it's better not to go.

But for me, there's no place like it. As the English author Samuel Johnson said, 'When a man is tired of London, he is tired of life.' And I simply have to agree.

Audioscript, exercise 1, page 49

Good morning, and welcome. I'm Alice Howe, your head teacher, and I'm here today to give you some advice about study skills as you start in the sixth form.

One of the main differences is that in the sixth form you have fewer subjects, but hopefully these are things that you personally are more interested in and have chosen to study. You'll have more time to spend on each of them, but you'll also have to work more independently.

This means that time management – is everyone clear what I mean by time management? – is very important. Make a note of deadlines and plan your work accordingly. Use lists to tick off assignments – homework, exercises, essays and so on - when you finish them, and remember that it's better to study and review on a regular basis than to leave it all to revision just before the exams. It's easy to leave things till the last minute. Remember that in the sixth form you'll also have opportunities to do other optional activities, get a part-time job or learn to drive – as well as having a busy social life. The better you organize your time, the more things you'll be able to do.

Effective research is a very important skill. Now, what do I mean by effective research? Well, what I'm talking about is organized study. It's easy to waste a lot of time, and it's also easy to get distracted when using the internet. Try not to download page after page – be selective. It's also important to remember that not everything on the internet is true – pages like Wikipedia are created through collaboration, and no one checks the contents. Try to read, think critically and then take notes. If you do this, you'll be expressing your own ideas rather than someone else's.

Note-taking is in itself a very important skill. There's no one correct way to do this – you have to find what suits you. Some people write detailed notes using full sentences. Others note key words or write the most important information using bullet points. More visual learners may prefer to use mind maps. It doesn't matter. The important thing is that it works for you and provides a summary of the main information which you can use for revision.

Exercise 5, page 55

Student A

Turn 1

- Your personal details appear below.
  James Martin
  32 Fleet Avenue
  London SW 1 3PT
- Listen carefully to Student B, he/she must check your details and correct any information that is wrong.

Turn 2

- Check your partner's personal details. This is what you think they are.
  Linda Barker
  14 King Street West
  Bath BA4 6FD
- Go through each line slowly. Remember to check by asking questions like *So your name's Linda...Barker...?*

Exercise 4, page 74

Job A

Title: Taxi driver

- autonomous – you can arrange your own working hours
- you earn according to your effort
- no boss or company to take any of the money
- opportunity to talk to lots of people
- long working hours
- stressful driving conditions
- not well paid once you've paid for petrol, car maintenance
- occasional danger from strange passengers

Job B

Title: Photographer

- creative, artistic job
- independent work
- interesting environment
- lack of job security, no regular income, no sick pay or holiday pay
- a lot of the job isn't glamorous
- a lot of waiting around
- lots of competition from other photographers

Speaking task, exercise 9, page 59

Student B

Compare and contrast the photos. Describe what you can see and how you think the people are feeling.

1

2

Exercise 5, page 55

Student B

Turn 1

- Check Student A's personal details. This is what you think they are.
  James Marvin
  31 Fleet Road
  London SW4 3CT

- Go through each line slowly, checking e.g. *So your name's James Marvin...?*

Turn 2

- Now Student A is going to check. This is your name.
  Lindsay Parker
  14 King Street East
  Bath BA6 6FB

- Listen carefully while A checks your details and correct any information that he/she has wrong.

Speaking task, exercises 2 and 3, page 86

Student B

Trains to Bath depart from London Paddington mainline station

Morning departures	9.30	10.00	10.30	11.00 etc
Morning arrival	10.59	11.24	11.59	12.24 etc
Departure platform	12	8	12	8
Return departures	15.13	15.43	16.13	16.43 etc
Return arrival	16.44	17.14	17.44	18.14 etc
Departure platform	1	1	1	1

Single adult fare £22   Return adult fare £39.50

Coaches to Bath from London Victoria Coach Station

Morning departures	8.00	9.30	10.00*	11.00
Morning arrival	11.20	12.50	13.47*	14.30
Departure bay	6	6	8	6

*this service involves a change of bus & 30 minute wait at Bristol

Return departures	12.00	13.45	15.00*	15.45
Return arrival	15.35	17.35	19.15*	19.20
Departure bay	4	4	4	4

*this service involves a change and a 45 minute wait in Bristol

Single adult coach fare £17.50   Return adult coach fare £28.00

Student A

Trains to York depart from Manchester Piccadilly mainline station as follows:

Morning departures	8.26	8.55	9.26	9.57
Morning arrival	9.55	10.23	10.52	11.23
Departure platform	4	8	4	4
Return departures	15.28	15.40*	15.58	16.28
Return arrival	16.49	17.09*	17.25	17.49
Departure platform	2	2	2	2

*returns to Manchester Oxford Road station

Single adult fare £22   Return adult fare £39.50

Coaches to York from Manchester Coach Station

Morning departures	8.30	8.45	
Morning arrival	11.50	12.00	
Departure bay	4	8	
Return departures	15.30	17.30	19.30
Return arrival	18.05	20.05	22.05
Departure bay	6	6	6

Single adult coach fare £9.80   Return adult coach fare £15.90

Speaking task, exercise 6, page 89

Student B

Talk about photos A and B. Discuss their similarities and differences and say how you think the people feel. Which situation would you prefer to be in?

Wordlist

Unit 1
Describing people
can't stand /ˌkɑːnt ˈstænd/
depressive /dɪˈpresɪv/ adj
emo /ˈiːməʊ/ adj
fun-loving /ˈfʌnˌlʌvɪŋ/ adj
goth /ɡɒθ/ n
hard-working /ˌhɑːdˈwɜːkɪŋ/ adj *
heavy /ˈhevi/ adj **
intense /ɪnˈtens/ adj **
introvert /ˈɪntrəvɜːt/ n
mate /meɪt/ n **
messy /ˈmesi/ adj
outgoing /ˌaʊtˈɡəʊɪŋ/ adj
(be) a pain /ˌ(biː) ə ˈpeɪn/
(be) a real laugh /ˌ(biː) ə rɪəl ˈlɑːf/
(be) not really bothered about /ˌ(bi) nɒt rɪəli ˈbɒðəd əbaʊt/
(be) quite keen on /ˌ(bi) kwaɪt ˈkiːn ɒn/
(be) really into /ˌ(bi) rɪəli ˈɪntuː/
relaxed /rɪˈlækst/ adj *
reserved /rɪˈzɜːvd/ adj
skater /ˈskeɪtə/ n
sporty /ˈspɔːti/ adj
strict /strɪkt/ adj **
understanding /ˌʌndəˈstændɪŋ/ adj
unreliable /ˌʌnrɪˈlaɪəbl/ adj *

Discussing relationships
classmate /ˈklɑːsmeɪt/ n
a girl from my class /ə ˌɡɜːl frəm maɪ ˈklɑːs/
judo /ˈdʒuːdəʊ/
a mutual friend /ə ˌmjuːtʃuəl ˈfrend/
neighbour /ˈneɪbə/ n ***
one of my parents' friends /ˌwʌn əv maɪ ˌpeərənts ˈfrendz/
the orchestra /ˌðiː ˈɔːkɪstrə/ n **
someone I know from (football) /ˌsʌmwʌn aɪ ˌnəʊ frəm (ˈfʊtbɔːl)/

Social networking
account /əˈkaʊnt/ n ***
acronym /ˈækrənɪm/ n
click on /ˈklɪk ˌɒn/ phr v *
confirm /kənˈfɜːm/ v ***
create /kriˈeɪt/ v ***
email address /ˈiːmeɪl əˌdres/ n ***
go to /ˈɡəʊ ˌtuː/ phr v
join /dʒɔɪn/ v ***
limit /ˈlɪmɪt/ v ***
netspeak /ˈnetˌspiːk/ n
online profile /ˌɒnlaɪn ˈprəʊfaɪl/ n
password /ˈpɑːsˌwɜː(r)d/ n *
question forum /ˈkwestʃ(ə)n ˌfɔːrəm/ n
register button /ˈredʒɪstə ˌbʌtn/ n
restrict /rɪˈstrɪkt/ v **
security question /sɪˈkjʊərəti ˌkwestʃ(ə)n/ n
set up /ˌset ˈʌp/ phr v
social interaction /ˌsəʊʃl ɪntərˈækʃn/ n
social networking site /ˌsəʊʃl ˈnetwɜːkɪŋ saɪt/ n
technophobe /ˈteknəʊfəʊb/ n
upload /ʌpˈləʊd/ v

Unit 2
Leaving school
A levels /ˈeɪ ˌlevlz/ n
apply for /əˈplaɪ fɔː/ v ***
apprenticeships /əˈprentɪsʃɪps/ n pl
degree /dɪˈɡriː/ n ***
enrol on /ɪnˈrəʊl ˌɒn/ v
further education /ˌfɜːðə edjuˈkeɪʃn/ n
placement /ˈpleɪsmənt/ n
qualifications /ˌkwɒlɪfɪˈkeɪʃənz/ n ***
recruit /rɪˈkruːt/ v **
sandwich course /ˈsændwɪdʒ ˌkɔːs/ n
school leaver /ˌskuːl ˈliːvəz/ n
sixth form /ˈsɪksθ ˌfɔːm/ n
sixth former /ˈsɪksθ ˌfɔːmə/ n
stay on /ˌsteɪ ˈɒn/ phr v
take on /ˌteɪk ˈɒn/ phr v
training course /ˈtreɪnɪŋ ˌkɔːs/ n
vacancies /ˈveɪkənsiz/ n *
vocational training /vəʊˈkeɪʃn(ə)l ˈtreɪnɪŋ/ n
work experience /ˈwɜːk ɪkˌspɪəriəns/ n

School subjects
art /ɑːt/ n
biology /baɪˈɒlədʒi/ n *
business studies /ˈbɪznəs ˌstʌdɪz/ n
chemistry /ˈkemɪstri/ n **
citizenship /ˈsɪtɪznʃɪp/ n *
French /frentʃ/ n
Greek /ɡriːk/ n
health studies /ˈhelθ ˌstʌdɪz/ n
history /ˈhɪst(ə)ri/ n ***
history of music /ˌhɪst(ə)ri əv ˈmjuːzɪk/ n
humanities /hjuːˈmænətiz/ n pl
ICT /ˌaɪsiːˈtiː/ n
Latin /ˈlætɪn/ n
maths /mæθs/ n *
opt for /ˈɒpt ˌfɔː/ phr v **
option /ˈɒpʃn/ n ***
PE /ˌpiːˈiː/ n
physics /ˈfɪzɪks/ n **
primary /ˈpraɪməri/ n ***
sciences /ˈsaɪənsəz/ n pl ***
the British/Spanish system /ðə ˈbrɪtɪʃ ˈspænɪʃ ˌsɪstəm/ n
technical drawing /ˌteknɪkl ˈdrɔːɪŋ/ n

Unit 3
Study abroad
balance /ˈbæləns/ n ***
course fees /ˈkɔːs ˌfiːz/ n
deposit /dɪˈpɒzɪt/ n **
different food /ˌdɪfrənt ˈfuːd/
enrolment fee /ɪnˈrəʊlmənt ˌfiː/ n
feel homesick /ˌfiːl ˈhəʊmsɪk/
full board /ˌfʊl ˈbɔːd/ n
grant /ɡrɑːnt/ n ***
half board /ˌhɑːf ˈbɔːd/ n
hall of residence /ˌhɔːl əv ˈrezɪdəns/ n
host family /ˈhəʊst ˌfæmli/ n
learn about another culture /ˌlɜːn əbaʊt əˌnʌðə ˈkʌltʃə/
meet new people /ˌmiːt njuː ˈpiːpl/
miss friends /ˌmɪs ˈfrendz/
registration /ˌredʒɪˈstreɪʃn/ n **
self-catering /ˌselfˈkeɪtərɪŋ/
shared apartment /ˌʃeəd əˈpɑːtmənt/ n
too expensive /ˌtuː ɪkˈspensɪv/

Language schools
airport transfer /ˈeəpɔːt ˌtrænsfɜː/ n
business English /ˈbɪznəs ˌɪŋglɪʃ/ n
conversation classes /kɒnvəˈseɪʃn ˌklɑːsɪz/ n
daily timetable /ˌdeɪli ˈtaɪmteɪbl/ n
Director of Studies /dəˌrektə əv ˈstʌdɪz/ n
flexible /ˈfleksəbl/ adj **
general English /ˈdʒen(ə)rəl ˌɪŋglɪʃ/ n
(be) good for /ˌ(bi) ˈɡʊd fɔː/
(be) a great way of /ˌ(biː) ə ɡreɪt ˈweɪ əv/
group class /ˈɡruːp ˌklɑːs/ n
guided tours /ˌɡaɪdɪd ˈtʊəz/ n
a homely environment /ə ˌhəʊmli ɪnˈvaɪrənmənt/
host family member /ˈhəʊst ˌfæmli ˌmembə/ n
intensive course /ɪnˈtensɪv ˌkɔːs/ n
language school /ˈlæŋgwɪdʒ ˌskuːl/ n
language student /ˈlæŋgwɪdʒ ˌstjuːdənt/ n
level test /ˈlevl ˌtest/ n
most of all /ˌməʊst əv ˈɔːl/
native speaker /ˌneɪtɪv ˈspiːkə/ n *
optional /ˈɒpʃnəl/ adj *
outing /ˈaʊtɪŋ/ n
personal space /ˌpɜːsnəl ˈspeɪs/ n
receptionist /rɪˈsepʃnɪst/ n *
self-access centre /selfˈækses ˌsentə/ n
social programme /ˈsəʊʃl ˌprəʊɡræm/ n
sporting and cultural activities /ˌspɔːtɪŋ ən ˌkʌltʃ(ə)rəl ækˈtɪvətiz/

survival English /səˈvaɪvl ˌɪŋglɪʃ/ n

The thing I like about ... /ðə ˌθɪŋ aɪ ˈlaɪk əbaʊt/

wifi access /ˈwaɪfaɪ ˌækses/ n

young learners course /ˌjʌŋ ˈlɜːnəz ˌkɔːs/ n

Unit 4
Shopping

accessories /əkˈsesəriz/ n **

aisle /aɪl/ n

ATM (AmE) /ˌeɪtiːˈem/ n

cash point (BrE) /ˈkæʃ ˌpɔɪnt/ n

chemist /ˈkemɪst/ n **

convenience store /kənˈviːniəns ˌstɔː/ n

customer /ˈkʌstəmə/ n ***

electrical appliances /ɪˌlektrɪkl əˈplaɪənsəz/ n

factory outlet /ˈfæktri ˌaʊtlet/ n

food hall /ˈfuːd ˌhɔːl/ n

health food shop /ˌhelθ fuːd ˈʃɒp/ n

household item /ˌhaʊshəʊld ˈaɪtəm/ n

kitchenware /ˈkɪtʃənˌweə/ n

manager /ˈmænɪdʒə/ n ***

newsagent /ˈnjuːzˌeɪdʒənt/ n

perfumery /pəˈfjuːməri/ n

post office /ˈpəʊst ˌɒfɪs/ n **

pound shop /ˈpaʊnd ˌʃɒp/ n

price tag /ˈpraɪs ˌtæg/ n

receipt /rɪˈsiːt/ n**

shelf /ʃelf/ n **

shop assistant /ˈʃɒp əˌsɪstənt/ n

shoplifter /ˈʃɒpˌlɪftə/ n

stationer /ˈsteɪʃnə/ n

store detective /ˈstɔː dɪˌtektɪv/ n

supermarket /ˈsuːpəˌmɑːkɪt/ n **

trolley /ˈtrɒli/ n *

window shopper /ˈwɪndəʊ ˌʃɒpə/ n

Asking for information

bigger /ˈbɪgə/ adj ***

cash /kæʃ/ n ***

cheaper /ˈtʃiːpə/ adj ***

checkout /ˈtʃekaʊt/ n

credit card /ˈkredɪt ˌkɑːd/ n **

design /dɪˈzaɪn/ n ***

escalator /ˈeskəˌleɪtə/ n

feature /ˈfiːtʃə/ n ***

heavier /ˈheviə/ adj ***

lift (BrE) /lɪft/ n **

meeting point /ˈmiːtɪŋ ˌpɔɪnt/ n

memory capacity /ˈmemri kəˌpæsəti/ n

more modern /ˌmɔː ˈmɒd(ə)n/ adj

more traditional /ˌmɔː trəˈdɪʃn(ə)l/ adj

sound quality /ˈsaʊnd ˌkwɒləti/ n

special offer /ˌspeʃl ˈɒfə/ n

weight /weɪt/ n ***

Consumer rights

cash refund /ˈkæʃ ˌriːfʌnd/ n

complaint form /kəmˈpleɪnt ˌfɔːm/ n

consumer /kənˈsjuːmə/ n ***

consumer protection /kənˌsjuːmə prəˈtekʃn/ n

credit note /ˈkredɪt ˌnəʊt/ n

damaged goods /ˌdæmɪdʒd ˈgʊdz/ n pl

duty /ˈdjuːti/ n ***

exchange /ɪksˈtʃeɪndʒ/ n ***

exchange /ɪksˈtʃeɪndʒ/ v **

faulty /ˈfɔːlti/ adj

guarantee /ˌgærənˈtiː/ n **

manufacturer /ˌmænjʊˈfæktʃərə/ n ***

policy /ˈpɒləsi/ n ***

poor service /ˌpɔː ˈsɜːvɪs/ n

receipt /rɪˈsiːt/ n **

recordings /rɪˈkɔːdɪŋz/ n ***

rights /raɪts/ n ***

Unit 5
Describing a photo

amazing lights /əˌmeɪzɪŋ ˈlaɪts/

behind /bɪˈhaɪnd/ prep ***

booing /ˈbuːɪŋ/ n

breathtaking scenery /ˌbreθteɪkɪŋ ˈsiːnəri/

car horns /ˈkɑː ˌhɔːnz/ n

chanting /ˈtʃɑːntɪŋ/ n

cheering /ˈtʃɪərɪŋ/ n

crowded /ˈkraʊdɪd/ adj *

exciting /ɪkˈsaɪtɪŋ/ adj **

filthy /ˈfɪlθi/ adj *

frustrating /frʌˈstreɪtɪŋ/ adj *

holidaymakers /ˈhɒlɪdeɪˌmeɪkəz/ n

nature-lovers /ˈneɪtʃə ˌlʌvəz/ n

noisy /ˈnɔɪzi/ adj *

overcrowded /ˌəʊvəˈkraʊdɪd/ adj

packed /pækt/ adj *

paddling /ˈpædlɪŋ/ n

peaceful /ˈpiːsfl/ adj **

pitch /pɪtʃ/ n **

pollution /pəˈluːʃn/ n ***

powerful sound-system /ˌpaʊəfl ˈsaʊnd sɪstəm/ n

serene /səˈriːn/ adj

shoreline /ˈʃɔːlaɪn/ n

smoky /ˈsməʊki/ adj

spray /spreɪ/ n *

stadium /ˈsteɪdiəm/ n *

at a standstill /ˌət ə ˈstændstɪl/

stressful /ˈstresfl/ adj

sunshade /ˈsʌnʃeɪd/ n

supporters /səˈpɔːtəz/ n ***

tense /tens/ adj *

unspoilt /ʌnˈspɔɪlt/ adj

Giving your opinion about a town/city

aspect /ˈæspekt/ n ***

commuters /kəˈmjuːtəz/ n *

congestion /kənˈdʒestʃ(ə)n/ n

fast-moving /ˈfɑːstˌmuːvɪŋ/ adj

good prospects of employment /ˌgʊd prɒspekts əv ɪmˈplɔɪmənt/

headquarters of organizations and businesses /hedˌkwɔːtəz əv ˌɔːgənaɪˌzeɪʃənz ənd ˈbɪznəsəz/

high pressure /ˌhaɪ ˈpreʃə/ n

international communications hub /ˌɪntəˌnæʃn(ə)l kəˈmjuːnɪkeɪʃ(ə)nz hʌb/ n

local public transport network /ˌləʊkl ˌpʌblɪk ˌtrɑːnspɔːt ˈnetwɜːk/ n

multicultural population /ˌmʌltɪˌkʌltʃərəl pɒpjʊˈleɪʃn/ n

range of leisure facilities /ˌreɪndʒ əv ˈleʒə fəsɪlətiz/

rush hour /ˈrʌʃ ˌaʊə/ n

seat of central government /ˌsiːt əv ˌsentrəl ˈgʌvnmənt/

a selection of universities and colleges /ə sɪˌlekʃn əv ˌjuːnɪˌvɜːsətiz ən ˈkɒlɪdʒəz/

sporting venue /ˈspɔːtɪŋ ˌvenjuː/ n

variety of entertainment options /vəˌraɪəti əv ˌentəˌteɪnmənt ˈɒpʃ(ə)nz/

Unit 6
Leisure activities

aerobics /eəˈrəʊbɪks/ n

athletics /æθˈletɪks/ n *

badminton /ˈbædmɪntən/ n

bar /bɑː/ n ***

basketball /ˈbɑːskɪtˌbɔːl/ n *

a bit of fun /ə ˌbɪt əv ˈfʌn/

a clear set of rules /ə ˌklɪə set əv ˈruːlz/

court /kɔːt/ n ***

cycling /ˈsaɪklɪŋ/ n

darts /dɑːts/ n

develop muscle tone /dɪˌveləp ˈmʌsl təʊn/

expend energy /ɪkˌspend ˈenədʒi/

football /ˈfʊtˌbɔːl/ n ***

give up /ˌgɪv ˈʌp/ phr v

gym /dʒɪm/ n *

hockey /ˈhɒki/ n *

ice skating /ˈaɪs ˌskeɪtɪŋ/ n

improve stamina /ɪmˌpruːv ˈstæmɪnə/

martial arts /ˌmɑːʃl ˈɑːts/ n *

modern dance /ˌmɒd(ə)n ˈdɑːns/ n

mountains /ˈmaʊntɪnz/ n ***

park /pɑːk/ n ***

physical effort /ˌfɪzɪkl ˈefət/ n

pick up /ˌpɪk ˈʌp/ phr v

Pilates /pəˈlɑːtiːz/ n

pool /puːl/ n ***

running /ˈrʌnɪŋ/ n **

sign up for /ˌsaɪn ˈʌp fɔː/ phr v

skating /ˈskeɪtɪŋ/ n *

skiing /ˈskiːɪŋ/ n

snooker /ˈsnuːkə/ n

spinning /ˈspɪnɪŋ/ n

squash /skwɒʃ/ n

stick at /ˈstɪk ˌæt/ phr v

swimming /ˈswɪmɪŋ/ n *

take part in /ˌteɪk ˈpɑːt ɪn/ phr v
take up /ˌteɪk ˈʌp/ phr v
tenpin bowling /ˌtenpɪn ˈbəʊlɪŋ/ n
track /træk/ n ***
weight training /ˈweɪt ˌtreɪnɪŋ/ n
work out /ˌwɜːk ˈaʊt/ phr v
yoga /ˈjəʊgə/ n

Unit 7
Advertising
ad /æd/ n
advertise /ˈædvətaɪz/ v **
advertisement /ədˈvɜːtɪsmənt/ n **
advertiser /ˈædvətaɪzə/ n
advertising agency /ˈædvətaɪzɪŋ ˈeɪdʒənsi/ n
brand name /ˈbrænd ˌneɪm/ n *
(advertising) campaign /(ˌædvətaɪzɪŋ) kæmˈpeɪn/ n ***
be catchy /ˌbi ˈkætʃi/
classified ad /ˌklæsɪfaɪd ˈæd/ n
commercial /kəˈmɜːʃl/ n *
commercial break /kəˌmɜːʃl ˈbreɪk/ n
consume /kənˈsjuːm/ v **
consumer /kənˈsjuːmə/ n ***
consumption /kənˈsʌmpʃn/ n **
encourage brand loyalty /ɪnˌkʌrɪdʒ ˌbrænd ˈlɔɪəlti/
flyer /ˈflaɪə/ n
get an idea across /ˌget ən aɪˌdɪə əˈkrɒs/
hoarding /ˈhɔːdɪŋ/ n
jingle /ˈdʒɪŋgl/ n
launch /lɔːntʃ/ v ***
logo /ˈləʊgəʊ/ n *
make an impact /ˌmeɪk ən ˈɪmpækt/
the (teenage) market /ðə ˌ(tiːneɪdʒ) ˈmɑːkɪt/ n
online advert /ˌɒnlaɪn ˈædvɜːt/ n
pop-up /ˈpɒpˌʌp/ n
poster /ˈpəʊstə/ n **
produce /prəˈdjuːs/ v ***
producer /prəˈdjuːsə/ n ***
product /ˈprɒdʌkt/ n ***
production /prəˈdʌkʃn/ n ***
promote /prəˈməʊt/ v ***
promoter /prəˈməʊtə/ n *
promotion /prəˈməʊʃn/ n ***
raise brand awareness /ˌreɪz brænd əˈweənəs/
slogan /ˈsləʊgən/ n *
sponsor /ˈspɒnsə/ n *
sponsor /ˈspɒnsə/ v **
sponsorship /ˈspɒnsəʃɪp/ n *

Advertising and health
controversial /ˌkɒntrəˈvɜːʃl/ adj **
devastating /ˈdevəsteɪtɪŋ/ adj *
be directed at /bi dəˈrektəd æt/
exploit /ɪkˈsplɔɪt/ v **
be exposed to /ˌbi ɪkˈspəʊzd tuː/
fast food /ˌfɑːst ˈfuːd/ n *
influence /ˈɪnfluːəns/ v ***

junk food /ˈdʒʌŋk ˌfuːd/ n
the media /ðə ˈmiːdiə/ n ***
obesity /əʊˈbiːsəti/ n
product placement /ˈprɒdʌkt ˌpleɪsmənt/ n
stimulate debate /ˌstɪmjʊleɪt dɪˈbeɪt/

Unit 8
Studying
assess /əˈses/ **
assignment /əˈsaɪnmənt/ n **
attentive /əˈtentɪv/ adj
average mark /ˌæv(ə)rɪdʒ ˈmɑːk/ n
balance of exams and coursework /ˌbæləns əv ɪgˌzæmz ən ˈkɔːswɜːk/
bullet points /ˈbʊlɪt ˌpɔɪnts/ n
class /klɑːs/ n ***
colour-coded notes /ˌkʌlə kəʊdəd ˈnəʊts/
condense your notes /kənˌdens jə ˈnəʊts/
continuous assessment /kənˌtɪnjʊəs əˈsesmənt/ n
coursework /ˈkɔːsˌwɜːk/ n
dedicated /ˈdedɪˌkeɪtɪd/ adj *
detailed notes /ˌdiːteɪld ˈnəʊts/ n
disappointed /ˌdɪsəˈpɔɪntɪd/ adj *
distraction /dɪˈstrækʃn/ n *
evaluate /ɪˈvæljueɪt/ v **
flexible /ˈfleksəbl/ adj **
frequency of exams /ˌfriːkwənsi əv ɪgˈzæmz/
grades /greɪdz/ n **
homework assignment /ˈhəʊmwɜːk əˌsaɪnmənt/ n
internet research /ˌɪntənet ˈriːsɜːtʃ/ n
jubilant /ˈdʒuːbɪlənt/ adj
mind map /ˈmaɪnd ˌmæp/ n
mock exam /ˈmɒk ˌɪgzæm/ n
note-taking /ˈnəʊtˌteɪkɪŋ/ n
optional activities /ˌɒpʃnəl ækˈtɪvətiz/ n
overwhelmed /ˌəʊvəˈwelmd/ adj
plagiarize /ˈpleɪdʒəraɪz/ v
research /rɪˈsɜːtʃ; ˈriːsɜːtʃ/ v ***
re-take /ˈriːteɪk/ n
review /rɪˈvjuː/ v ***
revision /rɪˈvɪʒn/ n **
speed reading /ˈspiːd ˌriːdɪŋ/ n
stressed /strest/ adj
summary /ˈsʌməri/ n **
timetable /ˈtaɪmˌteɪbl/ n **
uniform /ˈjuːnɪfɔːm/ n **
visual clues /ˌvɪʒʊəl ˈkluːz/ n
visual learners /ˌvɪʒʊəl ˈlɜːnəz/ n
visuals /ˈvɪʒʊəlz/ n
work independently /ˌwɜːk ɪndɪˈpendəntli/

Unit 9
On the road
bus lane /ˈbʌs ˌleɪn/ n
confident driver /ˌkɒnfɪd(ə)nt ˈdraɪvə/ n

congestion charge /kənˈdʒestʃ(ə)n ˌtʃɑːdʒ/ n
cycle lane /ˈsaɪkl ˌleɪn/ n
dangerous driver /ˌdeɪndʒərəs ˈdraɪvə/ n
driving instructor /ˈdraɪvɪŋ ɪnˌstrʌktə/ n
driving lessons /ˈdraɪvɪŋ ˌlesənz/ n
driving licence /ˈdraɪvɪŋ ˌlaɪsəns/ n
driving test /ˈdraɪvɪŋ ˌtest/ n
fine /faɪn/ n **
full driving licence /fʊl ˈdraɪvɪŋ ˌlaɪsəns/ n
fully-qualified driver /ˌfʊli ˌkwɒlɪfaɪd ˈdraɪvə/ n
give way /ˌgɪv ˈweɪ/
highway code /ˌhaɪweɪ ˈkəʊd/ n
jump the lights /ˌdʒʌmp ðə ˈlaɪts/
learner driver /ˌlɜːnə ˈdraɪvə/ n
L-plate /ˈelpleɪt/ n
no entry /ˌnəʊ ˈentri/
one way street /ˌwʌn weɪ ˈstriːt/ n
parking ticket /ˈpɑːkɪŋ ˌtɪkɪt/ n
pavement (BrE) /ˈpeɪvmənt/ n **
pedestrianized area /pəˌdestriənaɪzd ˈeəriə/ n
provisional driving licence /prəˌvɪʒnəl ˈdraɪvɪŋ laɪsəns/ n
right-hand drive /ˌraɪthænd ˈdraɪv/ n
road rage /ˈrəʊd ˌreɪdʒ/ n
roundabout /ˈraʊndəˌbaʊt/ n *
sidewalk (AmE) /ˈsaɪdˌwɔːk/ n
speed limit /ˈspiːd ˌlɪmɪt/ n
subway /ˈsʌbˌweɪ/ n
traffic jam /ˈtræfɪk dʒæm/ n
traffic lights /ˈtræfɪk ˌlaɪts/ n pl
traffic warden /ˈtræfɪk ˌwɔːdn/ n
zebra crossing /ˌzebrə ˈkrɒsɪŋ/ n

Directions
architecture /ˈɑːkɪtektʃə/ n **
galleries /ˈgæləriz/ n **
hot spring /ˌhɒt ˈsprɪŋ/ n
museums /mjuːˈziːəmz/ n ***
Romans /ˈrəʊmənz/ n
spa /spɑː/ n
tourist destination /ˈtʊərɪst destɪˌneɪʃn/ n
tourist information office /ˌtʊərɪst ɪnfəmeɪʃn ˈɒfɪs/ n
UNESCO World Heritage Site /juːˌneskəʊ wɜːld ˈherɪtɪdʒ saɪt/ n

Unit 10
Describing a photo
balding /ˈbɔːldɪŋ/ adj
chubby cheeks /ˌtʃʌbi ˈtʃiːks/ n
cropped /krɒpt/ adj
curly hair /ˌkɜːli ˈheə/ n
curvy /ˈkɜːvi/ adj
elderly /ˈeldəli/ adj ***
freckles /ˈfreklz/ n
(be) in her teens /(ˌbi) ɪn hə ˈtiːnz/

(be) in his early/middle/late twenties /
  (ˌbiː) ɪn hɪz ˌɜːli/ˌmɪdl/ˌleɪt ˈtwentiz/
laughter lines /ˈlɑːftə ˌlaɪnz/ n pl
middle-aged /ˌmɪdlˈeɪdʒd/ adj *
mole /məʊl/ n *
overweight /ˌəʊvəˈweɪt/ adj
piercing /ˈpɪəsɪŋ/ n
scar /skɑː/ n *
shoulder-length /ˈʃəʊldə ˌleŋθ/ adj
slim /slɪm/ adj **
straight /streɪt/ adj **
tattoo /tæˈtuː/ n
toddler /ˈtɒdlə/ n *
twinkling eyes /ˌtwɪŋklɪŋ ˈaɪz/ n
wavy /ˈweɪvi/ adj
well-built /ˌwelˈbɪlt/ adj
wrinkles /ˈrɪŋkəlz/ n

Fame and success
autograph hunter /ˈɔːtəgrɑːf ˌhʌntə/ n
award-winning /əˈwɔːdˌwɪnɪŋ/ adj
best-seller /ˌbestˈselə/ n
blockbuster /ˈblɒkˌbʌstə/ n
celebrity /səˈlebrəti/ n *
column /ˈkɒləm/ n ***
famous /ˈfeɪməs/ adj ***
fan /fæn/ n **
gold medallist /ˌgəʊld ˈmedlɪst/ n
gossip /ˈgɒsɪp/ n
hit series /ˌhɪt ˈsɪəriːz/ n
notorious /nəʊˈtɔːriəs/ adj *
one-hit wonder /ˌwʌnhɪt ˈwʌndə/ n
paparazzi /ˌpæpəˈrætsi/ n
platinum album /ˌplætɪnəm ˈælbəm/ n
star /stɑː/ n ***

Unit 11
Food
acidic /əˈsɪdɪk/ adj
bacon and eggs /ˌbeɪkən ən ˈegz/ n
balanced /ˈbælənst/ adj *
bangers and mash /ˌbæŋəz ən
  ˈmæʃ/ n
bitter /ˈbɪtə/ adj **
bread and butter /ˌbred ən ˈbʌtə/ n
cup and saucer /ˌkʌp ən ˈsɔːsə/ n
curry /ˈkʌri/ n
dark chocolate /ˌdɑːk ˈtʃɒklət/ n
dish /dɪʃ/ n **
exotic /ɪgˈzɒtɪk/ adj *
fast food restaurant /ˌfɑːst fuːd
  ˈrest(ə)rɒnt/ n
fish and chips /ˌfɪʃ ən ˈtʃɪps/ n *
food allergies /ˈfuːd ˌælədʒɪz/ n
fresh orange juice /freʃ ˈɒrɪndʒ
  dʒuːs/ n
greasy /ˈgriːsi/ adj *
healthy /ˈhelθi/ adj ***
healthy diet /ˌhelθi ˈdaɪət/ n
heavy /ˈhevi/ adj ***
hot /hɒt/ adj ***
knife and fork /ˌnaɪf ən ˈfɔːk/ n

locally-produced /ˌləʊkli
  prəˈdjuːst/ adj
nuts /nʌts/ n **
processed /ˈprəʊsest/ adj
rich /rɪtʃ/ adj ***
salt and pepper /ˌsɔːlt ən ˈpepə/ n
sickly /ˈsɪkli/ adj
spicy /ˈspaɪsi/ adj
steak and kidney pie /ˌsteɪk ən ˌkɪdni
  ˈpaɪ/ n
strawberries and cream /ˌstrɔːb(ə)riz
  ən ˈkriːm/ n
sweet /swiːt/ adj ***
sweet tooth /ˌswiːt ˈtuːθ/ n
take away food /ˌteɪk əweɪ ˈfuːd/ n
vegan diet /ˌviːgən ˈdaɪət/ n
vegetarian /ˌvedʒəˈteəriən/ n

Restaurants
bill /bɪl/ n ***
biscuit (BrE) /ˈbɪskɪt/ n **
cheeseburger /ˈtʃiːzˌbɜːgə/ n
chips (BrE) /tʃɪps/ n **
cookie (AmE) /ˈkʊki/ n
drive through /ˈdraɪv ˌθruː/ adj
eat in /ˌiːt ˈɪn/ phr v
fizzy drinks /ˌfɪzi ˈdrɪŋks/ n
fries (AmE) /fraɪz/ n pl
ketchup /ˈketʃʌp/ n
main course /ˈmeɪn ˌkɔːs/ n
mustard /ˈmʌstəd/ n
portion /ˈpɔːʃn/ n **
ration /ˈræʃn/ n
regular /ˈregjʊlə/ adj ***
serving /ˈsɜːvɪŋ/ n *
starter /ˈstɑːtə/ n *
take out /ˌteɪk ˈaʊt/ phr v
tip /tɪp/ n **

Unit 12
Young workers' jobs
24/7 /ˌtwentifɔː ˈsevn/
assistant /əˈsɪstənt/ n **
au pair /ˌəʊ ˈpeə/ n
authority /ɔːˈθɒrəti/ n ***
babysitter /ˈbeɪbɪˌsɪtə/ n *
barman /ˈbɑːmən/ n
barwoman /ˈbɑːwʊmən/ n
boss /bɒs/ n ***
(be) on call /(ˌbiː) ɒn ˈkɔːl/
camp counsellor /ˌkæmp
  ˈkaʊns(ə)lə/ n
cash in hand /ˌkæʃ ɪn ˈhænd/
clerical assistant /ˈklerɪkl əˌsɪstənt/ n
colleague /ˈkɒliːg/ n ***
contact with other people /ˌkɒntækt
  wɪð ˌʌðə ˈpiːpl/
CV (BrE) /ˌsiːˈviː/ n *
earn money /ˌɜːn ˈmʌni/
employee /ɪmˈplɔɪiː/ n ***
employer /ɪmˈplɔɪə/ n ***
employment /ɪmˈplɔɪmənt/ n ***

fast food attendant /ˌfɑːst ˈfuːd
  əˌtendənt/ n
football coach /ˈfʊtbɔːl ˌkəʊtʃ/ n
free admission tickets /ˌfriː ədˈmɪʃn
  tɪkɪts/ n
full-time work /ˌfʊltaɪm ˈwɜːk/ n
get work experience /get ˌwɜːk
  ɪkˈspɪəriəns/
holiday job (BrE) /ˈhɒlədeɪ ˌdʒɒb/ n
hours /aʊəz/ n ***
kitchen worker /ˈkɪtʃən ˌwɜːkə/ n
leader /ˈliːdə/ n ***
learn to be responsible /ˌlɜːn tə bi
  rɪˈspɒnsəbl/
lifeguard /ˈlaɪfˌgɑːd/ n
National Insurance contributions
  /ˌnæʃn(ə)l ɪnˌʃʊərəns
  kɒntrɪˈbjuːʃ(ə)nz/ n
newspaper boy/girl /ˈnjuːzpeɪpə ˌbɔɪ/
  ˌgɜːl/ n
night shifts /ˈnaɪt ˌʃɪfts/ n
owner /ˈəʊnə/ n ***
part-time job /ˌpɑːt taɪm ˈdʒɒb/ n
part-time work /ˌpɑːt taɪm ˈwɜːk/ n
pay and conditions
  /ˌpeɪ ən kənˈdɪʃ(ə)nz/ n
petrol pump attendant /ˌpetrəl pʌmp
  əˈtendənt/ n
pizza deliverer /ˈpiːtsə dɪˌlɪv(ə)rə/ n
pizza delivery person
  /ˌpiːtsə dɪˌlɪv(ə)ri ˈpɜːsn/ n
previous experience /ˌpriːviəs
  ɪkˈspɪəriəns/ n
repetitive work /rɪˌpetətɪv ˈwɜːk/ n
requirements /rɪˈkwaɪəmənts/ n ***
responsibility /rɪˌspɒnsəˈbɪləti/ n ***
résumé (AmE) /ˈrezjuːmeɪ/ n
Saturday job /ˈsætədeɪ ˌdʒɒb/ n
save up for /ˌseɪv ˈʌp fɔː/ phr v
shelf stacker /ˈʃelf ˌstækə/ n
shop assistant /ˈʃɒp əˌsɪstənt/ n
ski instructor /ˈskiː ɪnˌstrʌktə/ n
spending money /ˌspendɪŋ ˈmʌni/ n
stress /stres/ n ***
tax /tæks/ n ***
team member /ˈtiːm ˌmembə/ n
theme park attendant /ˌθiːm pɑːk
  əˈtendənt/ n
vacation work (AmE) /vəˈkeɪʃn
  ˌwɜːk/ n
waiter /ˈweɪtə/ n *
work in a team /ˌwɜːk ɪn ə ˈtiːm/

Unit 13
Experiences
backpacking /ˈbækˌpækɪŋ/ n
break /breɪk/ n ***
change your attitude /ˌtʃeɪndʒ jər
  ˈætɪtjuːd/
change your perspective on life /
  ˌtʃeɪndʒ jə pəˌspektɪv ɒn ˈlaɪf/
change your view of the world /
  ˌtʃeɪndʒ jə ˈvjuː əv ðə wɜːld/

defer /dɪˈfɜː/ v

a real eye-opener /ə ˌrɪəl ˈaɪəʊp(ə)nə/ n

gap year /ˈgæp ˌjɪə/ n

hitchhiking /ˈhɪtʃˌhaɪkɪŋ/ n

inter-railing /ˈɪntəˌreɪlɪŋ/ n

journey /ˈdʒɜː(r)ni/ n ***

life experience /ˈlaɪf ɪkˌspɪərɪəns/ n

make a contribution /ˌmeɪk ə kɒntrɪˈbjuːʃn/

make a difference /ˌmeɪk ə ˈdɪfrəns/

make something count /ˌmeɪk sʌmθɪŋ ˈkaʊnt/

a once-in-a-lifetime experience /ə ˌwʌns ɪn ə ˌlaɪftaɪm ɪkˈspɪərɪəns/ n

school leavers /skuːl liːvəz/ n

take a year out /ˌteɪk ə jɪə ˈaʊt/

third world /ˌθɜːd ˈwɜːld/ n

travel /ˈtræv(ə)l/ v ***

travelling /ˈtræv(ə)lɪŋ/

trip /trɪp/ n ***

volunteering /ˌvɒlənˈtɪərɪŋ/ n

work experience /ˈwɜːk ɪkˌspɪərɪəns/ n

Erasmus

cultural exchange /ˌkʌltʃ(ə)rəl ɪksˈtʃeɪndʒ/ n

European Union /ˌjʊərəpiːən ˈjuːnjən/ n

exchange programme /ɪkˈstʃeɪndʒ ˈprəʊgræm/ n

hands-on approach /ˈhændzˌɒn əˌprəʊtʃ/ n

student residence /ˌstjuːdnt ˈrezɪd(ə)ns/ n

study abroad /ˌstʌdi əˈbrɔːd/ n

teaching styles /ˈtiːtʃɪŋ ˌstaɪlz/ n

university course /juːnɪˈvɜːsəti ˌkɔːs/ n

Unit 14
Travel

arrivals hall /əˈraɪvəlz ˌhɔːl/ n

baggage check (BrE) /ˈbægɪdʒ ˌtʃek/ n

baggage reclaim area /ˌbægɪdʒ riːkleɪm ˈeərɪə/ n

bus /bʌs/ n ***

coach /kəʊtʃ/ n **

destination /ˌdestɪˈneɪʃn/ n **

direct service /dɪˌrekt ˈsɜːvɪs/ n

direction of travel /dɪˌrekʃn əv ˈtrævl/ n

eastbound /ˈiːstˌbaʊnd/ adj

fare /feə/ n **

ferry /ˈferi/ n *

first class /ˌfɜːst ˈklɑːs/ adj *

journey time /ˈdʒɜːni ˌtaɪm/ n

left luggage office (AmE) /left ˈlʌgɪdʒ ɒfɪs/ n

mainline station /ˌmeɪnlaɪn ˈsteɪʃn/ n

non-stop service /ˌnɒnstɒp ˈsɜːvɪs/ n

outward journey /ˌaʊtwəd ˈdʒɜːni/ n

overground /ˈəʊvəˌgraʊnd/ n

Oyster card /ˈɔɪstə ˌkɑːd/ n

passport control /ˈpɑːspɔːt kənˈtrəʊl/ n

period return /ˌpɪərɪəd rɪˈtɜːn/ n

plane /pleɪn/ n ***

railcard /ˈreɪlˌkɑːd/ n

railroad (AmE) /ˈreɪlˌrəʊd/ n

rail-travellers' information centre /ˌreɪltræv(ə)ləz ɪnfəˈmeɪʃn ˈsentə/ n

railway (BrE) /ˈreɪlweɪ/ n ***

schedule (AmE) /ˈʃedjuːl/ n **

scheduled stops /ˈʃedjuːld ˈstɒps/ n

southbound /ˈsaʊθˌbaʊnd/ adj

stopping service /ˈstɒpɪŋ ˌsɜːvɪs/ n

street car (AmE) /ˈstriːt ˌkɑː/ n

student travel-card /ˈstjuːdnt ˈtrævlkɑːd/ n

subway (AmE) /ˈsʌbˌweɪ/ n

ticket machines /ˈtɪkɪt məˌʃiːnz/ n

timetable (BrE) /ˈtaɪmˌteɪbl/ n **

train /treɪn/ n ***

tram (BrE) /træm/ n

transport system /ˈtrænspɔːt ˌsɪstəm/ n

tube (BrE) /tjuːb/ n **

tube station /ˈtjuːb ˌsteɪʃn/ n

Underground (BrE) /ˈʌndəˌgraʊnd/ n

Reservations

advance booking /ədˌvɑːns ˈbʊkɪŋ/ n

aisle seat /ˈaɪl ˌsiːt/ n

bay /beɪ/ n **

book /bʊk/ v **

forward-facing seat /ˌfɔːwədˌfeɪsɪŋ ˈsiːt/ n

internet rate /ˈɪntənet ˌreɪt/ n

off-peak /ˌɒfˈpiːk/ adj

one way (AmE) /ˈwʌn ˌweɪ/ n

open ticket /ˌəʊpən ˈtɪkɪt/ n

platform /ˈplætˌfɔːm/ n **

reserve /rɪˈzɜːv/ v **

return (BrE) /rɪˈtɜːn/ n ***

round trip (AmE) /ˌraʊnd ˈtrɪp/ n

rush hour /ˈrʌʃ ˌaʊə/ n

single (BrE) /ˈsɪŋgl/ n **

stop /stɒp/ n **

telephone booking /ˈtelɪfəʊn ˌbʊkɪŋ/ n

validate your ticket /ˌvælɪdeɪt jə(r) ˈtɪkɪt/

window seat /ˈwɪndəʊ ˌsiːt/ n

Unit 15
Describing a photo

amazing performance /əˌmeɪzɪŋ pəˈfɔːməns/

backing singers /ˈbækɪŋ ˌsɪŋəz/ n

candidates /ˈkændɪdeɪts; ˈkændɪdəts/ n ***

concert /ˈkɒnsət/ n **

different generations /ˌdɪfrənt dʒenəˈreɪʃənz/

family celebration /ˈfæmli seləˈbreɪʃənz/ n

fans /fænz/ n **

get back in touch /ˌget bæk ɪn ˈtʌtʃ/

get-together /ˈgetˌtəgeðə/ n

grandstand /ˈgrændˌstænd/ n

great atmosphere /ˌgreɪt ˈætməsfɪə/ n

home crowd /ˌhəʊm ˈkraʊd/ n

invigilator /ɪnˈvɪdʒɪleɪtə/ n

keep an eye on the time /ˌkiːp ən ˌaɪ ɒn ðə ˈtaɪm/

nervous tension /ˌnɜːvəs ˈtenʃn/ n

play an encore /ˌpleɪ ən ˈɒŋkɔː/

public examination /ˌpʌblɪk ɪgzæmɪˈneɪʃn/ n

sporting event /ˈspɔːtɪŋ ɪˌvent/ n

stadium /ˈsteɪdɪəm/ n *

support band /səˈpɔːt ˌbænd/ n

wedding anniversary /ˈwedɪŋ ænɪˌvɜːs(ə)ri/ n

Having a formal debate

Affirmative speaker /əˈfɜːmətɪv ˈspiːkə/ n

Against /əˈgenst/ ***

argue against /ˈɑːgjuː əˌgenst/

content /ˈkɒntent/ n **

debate /dɪˈbeɪt/ n ***

debating /dɪˈbeɪtɪŋ/ n

For /fɔː/ ***

judge /dʒʌdʒ/ n ***

manner /ˈmænə/ n ***

marks /mɑːks/ n ***

matter /ˈmætə/ n ***

motion /ˈməʊʃn/ n ***

Negative speaker /ˌnegətɪv ˈspiːkə/ n

present an argument /prɪˌzent ən ˈɑːgjʊmənt/

speaker /ˈspiːkəz/ n ***

speech /spiːtʃ/ n ***

team /tiːm/ n ***

An event in Britain

amateur theatre groups /ˌæmətə ˈθɪətə gruːps/ n

buskers /ˈbʌskəz/ n

camping /ˈkæmpɪŋ/ n *

cosy venues /ˌkəʊzi ˈvenjuːz/ n

headline /ˈhedlaɪn/ v

international championship /ˌɪntəˌnæʃn(ə)l ˈtʃæmpɪənʃɪp/ n

knockout tournament /ˌnɒkaʊt ˈtʊənəmənt/ n

main stage /ˌmeɪn ˈsteɪdʒ/ n

street performers /ˈstriːt pəˌfɔːməz/ n

support act /səˈpɔːt ˌækt/ n

top level players /ˌtɒp levl ˈpleɪəz/ n

trophy /ˈtrəʊfi/ n **

Macmillan Education
Between Towns Road, Oxford OX4 3PP
A division of Macmillan Publishers Limited
Companies and representatives throughout the world

ISBN 978-0-230-44017-3 (Coursebook)
ISBN 978-0-230-44018-0 (Pack)

First edition published 2011
This edition published 2012

Design concept by Designers Collective
Designed by Calcium
Illustrated by John Haslam p8; Martin Sanders pp16, 54, 56,
78, 84, 86
Cover design by Designers Collective
Cover Credit: Superstock/Corbis, Superstock/Dream
Pictures/Shannon Faulk/Purestock, Superstock/Kablonk,
Superstock/Mother Image, Superstock/PhotoAlto.
Picture research by Catherine Dunn

Written by Kate Pickering

Kate would like to dedicate this book to the memory of
Gertrud Maus, whose passion for teaching and ability to
engage and enthuse a room full of indifferent sixth-formers
has been a life-long inspiration.

The author and publishers would like to thank the following
for permission to reproduce their photographs:
The Advertising Archives/Orange ad detail © Orange
p40(tr); **Alamy**/Adphotos p92(b), Alamy/Afripics.com pp29(c),
34(4), Alamy/Bubble Photography p5(cr), Alamy/Rory
Buckland p54(br), Alamy/Michelle Chaplow p33, Alamy/Ian
Dagnall p84(cr), Alamy/Denka Images p65(bcl) Alamy/Chris
Fertig p4(tl), Alamy/Peter Fosberg p82(3), Alamy/David Gee
p5(br), Alamy/Jeff Greenberg p79(tr), Alamy/David Grossman
p72(tl), Alamy/Chris Howes/Wild Places p24, Alamy/i-Love
Images p61(background, br), Alamy/Imagebroker p83(tc),
Alamy/Imagepast p54(cl), Alamy/Imagesource p50(tl), Alamy/
Larry Lilac p37(heads,tails), Alamy/David Levenson p67(c),
Alamy/Liquid Light p54(cr), Alamy/MBI p23(tc), Alamy/
Oleksy Maksymenko Photography p26(tr), Alamy/Mauritius
Images GmbH p50(tr), Alamy/Mode Images p5(tm), Alamy/
Pjrstudio p79(cr), Alamy/Photoalto p37(tr), Alamy/Photolibrary
Wales p32(trc), Alamy/Photospin p49, Alamy/Photostudio.
com p84(tr), Alamy/Picture Scotland p93(t,cl), Alamy/
Premier p54(tl), Alamy/Radius images p5(tr), Alamy/Real
Image p85(tl), Alamy/Francis Roberts p90(tl), Alamy/Andrew
Rodriguez p12(br), Alamy/SFL Travel p85, Alamy/Alex Segre
p29(b), Alamy/Trevor Smithers ARPS p54(tr), Alamy/Kumar
Sriskandan p73, Alamy/John Warburton-Lee Photography
p83(tl), Alamy/Jim West p62|(tr), Alamy/Janine Wiedel
Photolibrary p88(tl), Alamy/Christophe Viseux p70(cr); **Apple
Inc**/i-phone p26(tr); **Bananastock** pp16(tr,c), 30(tr), 31, 32(tr),
34(3,5), 47, 53, 58(tr); **Bebo.com** p6(cr); **BrandX Pictures**
pp22(3), 25, 28(tr), 60(cr), 66(fries), 68, 71(2,3,4), 72(tr), 105;
Comstock Images pp64(4),106; **Chupa Chups** p40(tl)
courtesy of Parfetti Van Melle; **Corbis** pp4(4), 17(B), 19, 32(tl),
72(l), 77(tr), 96, 102; Corbis/Stewart Cohen/Pam Ostrow/
Blend Images p65(cr), Corbis/Claudia Gopper/Beyond
p12(cr), Corbis/Randy Ferris p91(ct,t), Corbis/Imagesource
p17(tr), Corbis/Erik Isakson p106, Corbis/Mika p76(cl),
Corbis/Moodboard p70(tr), Corbis/Michael Prince p76(tr),
Corbis/Radius Images p43, Corbis/Romeo Ranco/Reuters
p72(tc), Corbis/Hugh Sitton pp77(cl,cr), 80(tr), Corbis/Paul A
Souders p77(cm), Corbis/Neil Tingle p93(cr), Creatas p70(br),
Design Pics pp7, 63(6); **Digital Vision** pp4(1), 20, 46(B),
78(tl), 100, 103; **Eyewire** p13, Eyewire DDB Sydney p46(A);
Fancy p22(br); **Getty Images** pp10(Jo), 26(cl), 28(tl), 38, 41,
64(2,3,5), 66(ketchup, cola), 76(br), 82(2), 83(tr), 88(tr), 89(c,
background), 91(c), 90(tr), 92(A, C), 93(tr), Getty Images/
AFP p60(tr,br), Getty Images/Chelsea FC p89(br), Getty
Images/Commercial Eye p46(tcr), Getty Images/Full House
images p34(2), Getty Images/Fuse p67(tl), Getty Images/
Imagesource p14, Getty Images/India Today Group p91(cl),
Getty Images/Kevin Macintosh p18(cl,cr), Getty Images/
Angel Martinez p91(tr), Getty Images/Stockbyte p58(cr), Getty
Images/Ian Waldie p46(tr); **Goodshoot** pp36(tr), 84(tl); **Image
100** p52(2); **Imagesource** pp10(Gemma), 22(2), 52(5),56,
59, 64(1), 66(water); **Macmillan Education**/Paul Bricknall
p83(cr); **Myspace.com** p6(tr); **New South Wales Police** p44
(advertising image courtesy of NSW Police); **Penguin Books**
p42; **Photoalto** pp10(Dean), 11(Rhona), 82(1), 97, 105;
Photodisc pp4(3), 34(1). 36(tl), 59(1, background), 80(cr), 98,
101; **Photofusion**/Paul Doyle pp62(cl), 63(t): **Pixtal** pp52(6),
52(3), 51(1), 52(4), 99: **Photolibrary**/i-love Images p5(B),
Photolibrary/Imagebroker.net p23(tr); **Rex Features**/Olycom
SPA p40(tc); **Rubberball** pp22(1), 71(1): **Science Photo
Library** p23(tl); **Stockbyte** pp8, 11(Alex), 30(cr), 34, 78(tr),
95; Superstock pp12(tr), 74, Superstock/Corbis p1(crm),
94(brc), Superstock/Dream Pictures/Shannon Faulk pp1 (crl,
cll) 94(brl, bcl), **Superstock**/Kablonk pp1(bll,tll,cll),94(bll,tll),
Superstock/Mother Image pp1(clr),94(blr), Superstock/
Photoalto pp1(tlm,brb,brr,tlc), 94(tlm,brb,brr,tlc); **Tuenti**
p6(cbl); **Twitter.com** p6(cl).

These materials may contain links for third party websites.
We have no control over, and are not responsible for, the
contents of such third party websites. Please use care when
accessing them.

Although we have tried to trace and contact copyright
holders before publication, in some cases this has not been
possible. If contacted we will be pleased to rectify any errors
or omissions at the earliest opportunity.

Printed and bound in Spain by Edelvives

2016 2015 2014 2013 2012
10 9 8 7 6 5 4 3 2 1